Social Objects

Socially Engaged Craft Theory, Practice and Action

Socially Engaged Craft Collective

Published by Socially Engaged Craft Collective
Social Objects was produced in partnership with c3:initiative
and released during NCECA 2017 in in Portland, OR.

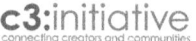

Cover images courtesy Flickr Commons
and Internet Archive Book Images.
No known copyright restrictions.

ISBN: 978-1543169782

Organized and edited by Mary Callahan Baumstark.
Organized and designed by Amanda Leigh Evans.

Table of Contents

Alex Amerri
Mariana Baquero
The Brick Factory
Rebecca Chernow
Keeryong Choi
Roz Crews
Henry James Haver Crissman
Jamie Crooke Powell
Jen DePaolo
Monica Dixon
Jeni Hansen Gard &
    Forrest Sincoff Gard
Brian Gillis
nicole gugliotti
Holly Hanessian
Gregory Hatch
Shannon Hebert Waldman
Ayumi Horie & Nick Moen
Max Infeld
Joshua Kosker
Kari Marboe
Mac McCusker & Project Canary
    (nicole gugliotti, Lauren Karle,
    & collaborators)
Lauren Moran
Hannah Newman
Salty (Xi Jie Ng)
Rosa Novak
Iviva Olenick
Lauren Sandler
Michael J. Strand
Robin Tieu (& Art + Feminism)
Brian Widmaier

Foreward

c3:initiative

The Socially Engaged Craft Collective's exhibition, Social Objects, represents the range of thoughtful intervention and community-building made possible through art that is centered around its public. The fourteen included artists are critically engaged with the labors of meticulously crafting objects, and giving equal care to the experiences produced around those objects. The presented projects range from the participatory to the contemplative in order to engineer perception-changing happenings from once banal-seeming encounters. c3:initiative is thrilled to support the exhibition of these works as well as the wealth of thoughtful context behind their making. This publication stands as a further artifact of the engagements and practices not easily encapsulated in static exhibition space as we've come to know it. These diligent makers, diverse in their crafts, aims, and cultural stakes, broaden the notion that contemporary craft has guarded constraints and limited effects.

About c3

c3:initiative is a platform for critical inquiry, dedicated to societal wellness through the production of contemporary art and integral conversation. We holistically support thinkers from various disciplines through the full arc of the creative process, prioritizing nascent and transitionary stage endeavors. Through use of two distinct campuses (one urban, one rural), c3 connects disparate communities and makerships through adaptive residency programs, a project incubator, community partnerships, and integrative public programming.

By providing various modes of infrastructural support for process-driven artist and academic projects, c3 offers forward-thinking models for collaboration and resource sharing. Our flexible programmatic calendar is committed to facilitating artistic partnerships, fostering community exchange, and developing educational opportunities through dialogue and increased visibility. c3's interdisciplinary approach to curiosity is committed to a freedom from quantifiable outcomes. Instead, c3:initiative proposes the radical space-making and flexibility necessary to illuminate community potential.

About the Exhibition

Social Objects emerges from partnership between the Socially Engaged Craft Collective (SECC) and c3:initiative in Portland, OR, resulting in an exhibition highlighting the intersection of socially engaged art and the ceramic medium. Social Objects runs concurrently with the 2017 National Conference on Education in the Ceramic Arts (NCECA), from March 23 - April 14, 2017. The opening reception on Thursday, March 23, features a variety of clay-based interactive projects, performances, and games that focused on collaboration with communities in Portland, both permanent and emergent.

Social Objects includes works from 14 members of the SECC, representing a wide range of practices, approaches, objects, and positionalities. Works such as Holly Hanessian's installation *Touch Sensorium*, invite visitors to explore tactile sensations through clay, while Forrest Sincoff Gard's *Waffle Toss,* a participatory pay-to-play game involving ceramic waffles and a foam toaster, encourages participants to toss, break, and play with ceramic objects. In Amanda Leigh Evans' *From and To Dust,* Evans explores both death and dying through a long-term collaborative urn project with individuals in the greater Portland area, and M.C. Baumstark utilizes both cocktails and souvenir, ceramic, menstrual cups to casually approach menstruation and its cultural connotations in her *Menstrual Cup Project*.

Other works move beyond c3's physical location such as Nicole Seisler's *Studio Souvenirs*, a series of pressed porcelain blocks that record specific moments in the artist's visit to Portland. Jeni Hansen Gard and Lauren Karle's *Weaving Dialogues*, a tea and conversation project that invites strangers to share an intimate conversation, guides participants with conversation prompts and questions left by previous participants, embroidered on a tablecloth. In Anna Metcalfe's *Upstream,* Metcalfe explores the people and places in the Willamette River Watershed though a cup exchange project, and nicole gugliotti's *10690 Wild Flowers*, honors the story of each person accessing abortion services in Oregon (10,690 individuals last year) and raises money for those who are denied access to reproductive healthcare in Oregon.

This exhibition, partnership, and networks speaks to the communicative power of ceramic objects and practices, in tandem with participatory and socially engaged art. These works vary in their degree of participation, but hold, at their core, a dedication to the social interstices made possible by art and craft. Participants are asked to consider the age-old relational capacity of ceramics and the futures made possible by socially engaged practices

The exhibition included work by Mary Callahan Baumstark, Henry Crissman & Hamilton Poe, Amanda Leigh Evans, nicole gugliotti, Holly Hanessian, Jeni Hansen Gard & Lauren Karle, Anna Metcalfe, Cheyenne Rudolph, Nicole Seisler, Forrest Sincoff Gard, Michael Strand, Juliette Walker, and Summer Zickefoose.

The works described by SECC within the *Social Objects* book do not necessarily reflect the works exhibited in Social Objects, the exhibition, given the experimental, exploratory, and participatory natures of many of these works. Authors were invited to describe previous projects or explore project futures.

Social Objects opened during NCECA 2017 at c3:initiative at 7326 N Chicago Ave, Portland, OR 97203 from March 23 - April 14, 2017.

About the Socially Engaged Craft Collective

The Socially Engaged Craft Collective (SECC) is an expanding network of artists who create a wide range of socially engaged art projects that are rooted in the history of craft objects and materials. The SECC aims to promote artists and to expose other artists, educators, and those who are interested to the wide spectrum of socially engaged craft. In addition to highlighting artists and their artwork, the SECC is an open resource of knowledge, news, and professional opportunities within the field.

On Theory

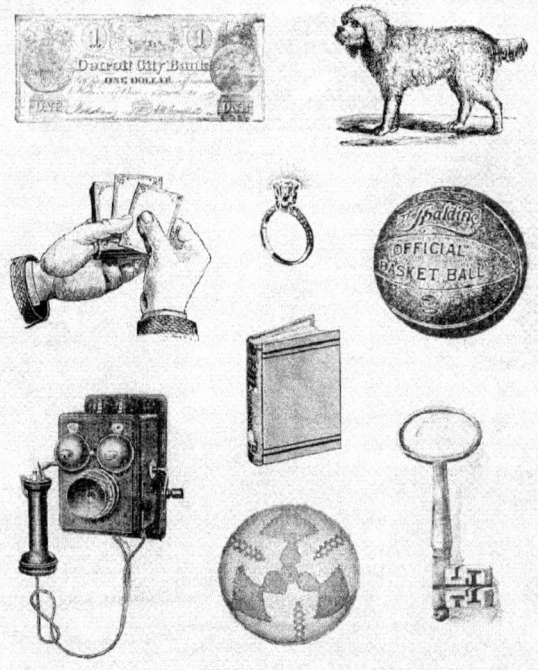

Meditations, complications, and reflections on
Socially Engaged Craft, its theories and practitioners.

Socialization vs. Social Objects

Namita Gupta Wiggers

When did you last socialize a puppy? It's a time sensitive endeavor with a short window of opportunity. During those early weeks, the puppy must be introduced to as many things as possible – socialized – to be comfortable with a range of types of people, surfaces, heights, kinds of water, noises, travel experiences, smells, and other animals.[1] The aim is, of course, to connect the puppy with anything and everything it might encounter, so that when it encounters it again later in life it will not be a surprise. Socialization is a process by which the unfamiliar becomes commonplace, a means of moving a living creature through social and material systems to normalize the new. While a puppy is not an object, there is something about the way in which an object is normalized – or not normalized – at play in the idea of a "social object."

Rivers of ink and forests of pages have been used up to address the relationship between humans and objects. We are consumed by stuff, overwhelmed by the objects we make, use, and discard. Nearly every discipline and a myriad of theoretical approaches address human/object relationships in some way, from Art History to Western Philosophy, Material Culture to Object Oriented Ontology. For a project, then, to add "social" to the word "object" implies something in addition to, something beyond daily interactions or commodity exchange to address systems through which humans encounter, employ, and engage objects. What, then, constitutes a successful "social object" in the world of clay? How does a project successfully shift from experiment to meaningful social interaction?

As an adjective, "social" defines something related to society or social systems. This clears space for the ceramic-based artist to address such networks, perhaps through user-centered design and the way in which the object invites engagement and use, or through systems of commodity exchange and layers of meaning an object accumulates through what Arjun Appadurai outlines as *The Social Life of Things*.[2] To use the word "social" with "object" moves the interaction between people and objects beyond a simple exchange or use of an object; it requires the interaction to address questions of collectivity, civil systems, and underlying meanings instigated and produced by communal gatherings. The circulatory nature of ceramic objects is evident at an everyday level. Human-made objects composed of clay are often employed in social rituals or interactions: an exchanged cup or bowl, a casserole dish used to present food at a shared meal, etc. Such physical items can connect to and reflect social structures around and through which they come into being, are circulated, collected, used to present food or drink, etc. However, the presence of a clay-based object within a social gathering is not enough to meet the responsibilities and opportunities of the "social object." A social object must do more work; it cannot merely circulate or act in tandem with social systems. A social object reveals how objects connect, reflect, and disrupt social systems.

It is in one of the definitions of "object" that this comes into view. Moving from understanding the object as a material form, something made, touched, seen, etc. to object as a verb brings out the way in which a "social object" pulls out of the mundane and everyday to call attention to both itself and social systems. To object is to express disapproval or disagreement, to call attention to something. A "social object," then, does not conform to social standards or normative expectations in its active state. In our evaluation of "social objects," a question needs to be asked: how does this object expand or push against the limits of social interaction in a way that gives the "social object" agency to be more than an object?

One of the most slippery aspects of a social object is tied up in proximity; ceramics requires proximity to materials, to the process of making an object, and in the use of that object. Haptic engagement is key – at the point of fabrication as much as reception, and those who work through clay employ any range of methods and techniques to highlight connections of physical touch between maker and user. While a bowl may show a fingerprint in the fired clay, or reveal itself in a circular unglazed spot, this mark of a maker does not make a bowl a social object.

Unless re-situated, destabilized or disruptive of social systems and norms in some way, any object remains a social-ized object, not a social object. By this I mean that it is like the puppy taken out on walks to meet, greet, and become comfortable with people. It is an object that circulates and moves within an approved system rather than an object that pushes social interaction into a new space, form, or a way to illuminate the frameworks of society itself. A social object must be a conduit for change – whether a small behavioral gesture or shift in a social norm or public action. For a social object to move within a collective is one thing – but for the same object to push against insularity and ensure movement between and across people and groups is a space of potential. This is where a social object can do its most effective work as an object and an action, a social object and a social object – a space beyond socialization in which there is potential to effect change.

Endnotes
1. Nancy Freedman-Smith, "Socialize Your Puppy," Life with Dogs, http://www.lifewithdogs.tv/2012/01/socialize-your-puppy-our-checklist-will-help/. Retrieved February 24, 2017.
2. See Arjun Appadurai, The Social Life of Things: Commodities in Cultural Perspective, (Cambridge University Press, Cambridge, UK, 1988).

Traversing Topographies: Craftivism and Socially Engaged Craft in Conversation

Mary Callahan Baumstark and Shannon Hebert Waldman

MARY: This is a question I get asked all the time, "What is the difference between socially engaged craft (SEC) and Craftivism?"[1] Can we solidly define them, and what are we accomplishing through this conversation?

SHANNON: When I was writing my thesis on Socially Engaged Craft (at Warren Wilson College)[2], I was trying to separate SEC from Craftivism because Craftivism had been defined as a movement rather than the methodology. I was still working within the parameters of both being movements.

MARY: Right. My Masters thesis[3] at OCAD University examined Craftivism as a way of working or method, rather than a concrete, artistic movement with a start and end. The use of the term "movement" is simplistic when we're looking at craft production in the 21st century. Everything is pretty nebulous. My definitions extend Craftivism to a variety of craft materials and processes, rather than limiting it to work defined as "craftivist" by previous writings as those artworks were all based in fiber and textiles. I often said, there's a reason we don't call it "Fiber-vism" or "Knit-a-vism." Craftivism is capable of moving beyond its history and early material limitations.

SHANNON: Yes! I see "social engagement" as a methodology, but I see Socially Engaged Art (SEA) or SEC as the artistic result.

MARY: Both SEA and SEC take "social engagement" as both their subject and material. SEC also incorporates craft products, processes, or materials as a second material or subject in addition to social engagement. Unlike SEC, Craftivism doesn't always necessitate engagement with a group of people, but it does always include an act of resistance against some sort of network, often an oppressive one.

We might be tempted to think of these engagements (both SEC and Craftivism) as inherently public. This public nature, for me, complicates the differences between SEC and Craftivism, especially after reading Johanna Hedva's "Sick Woman Theory."[4] There are people who don't have the same access to public life, such as people who are disabled, elderly. Hedva points out that these folks can still enact political moments within their lives. That being said, Craftivism is often social; resistance can be a communal activity. So many of the projects that came to define Craftivism-as-movement, or early Craftivism, were performed and created communally, and I think that's where the confusion between the two got started.

Many Craftivism projects are socially engaged and vice versa, so many SEC projects are political or activist in some way. There's a lot of social engagement that deals just with the relationships between other people, which are inherently political. Did

you find that artists were defining social engagement as activist or political in your research?

SHANNON: No. And that's what was interesting. The end
product was always be defined as a piece of art,
which is actually where critics, like Claire Bishop[5],
criticize SEA for being more social work than
a form of aesthetics. She argues that rather than
an aesthetic field, SEA is a social work field that
involves making, or something like Theatre of the
Oppressed, or art therapy.

That's a very relevant criticism in the SEA community that I don't think applies to the SEC
community as much, because the craft objects
are so inherently interactive, they are meant to be
used, as opposed to many art objects which do not
reference a utilitarian origin.

But, I do feel like the politics were definitely there. It
was just that they were never separated from the art.
So if you're asking, "is it marked as political?" No. It
was marked as art that was using political motivations
to maybe accomplish its aesthetic end goal.

If a community comes together to produce a work
of art, like Pablo Helguera's Liberas Donceles,
where he created a traveling library of Spanish
language books, the library isn't necessarily an
aesthetic piece, it's more of a community service.
The art world measures that by how is this aesthet-
ically valuable, rather than solely socially or polit-
ically valuable. But I'm unsure if the craft world is
defining the aesthetic component of the object as
having more or less merit than the singular political
act of Craftivism or Socially Engaged Craft. Does
that make sense?

MARY: Yes! Let's talk about objects. While craft is kind of a catch-all term, for process, practice, materials, products, the discipline is still object oriented.

Both SEC and Craftivism take the object as the catalyst, as this moment of understanding or change in an engagement, or in a relationship. These practices take objects that are inherently understandable to us; we are constantly surrounded by objects crafted or made in fiber or ceramic or wood or metal; objects that construct our domestic spaces. We have this instant moment of understanding, affect, and memory with craft objects and that can happen on a physical level, it can happen on an emotional level, but there is a real, shared, human history around craft objects that immediately connects us, as opposed to alienating us.

There is a potential for SEA and activist practices can be really alienating. At times performance can be alienating or frightening, protests can be claustrophobic and loud... Craftivism and SEC provide tangible, accessible counterpoints to these practices, and ground them in the objects or processes of craft.

SHANNON: Within craft practices (like SEC and Craftivism), objects also become important for their collectability and their physical evidence. The object is the catalyst for that engagement or interaction, but it's also the evidence or document of those relationships. With Craftivism or SEC, the focus is on how did this point of interaction change someone's mind or make them interact with each other in a different way.

Like the Cups of Conversation (Jeni Hansen Gard) or The Democratic Cup (organized by Nick Moen and Ayumi Horie), the act of having the conversation was the final piece, and the piece isn't accomplished without that, but the object of the cup is certainly necessary to get to that engagement.

What I find engaging about Craftivism and SEC is that both are incomplete without both an object and interaction. You can't have that interaction without the object but the object alone is stagnant without that engagement.

MARY: I would maybe couch the word "object" with both process and practice of craft. Namita Gupta Wiggers wrote this really wonderful essay called "Craft Performs,"[6] where she talks about the lineage of demonstration in craft and how craft objects, and the physical reminders of their process, things like stitches, throw lines, and fingerprints really speak to the artist's hand in a way that creates both an experience in the present moment but also in memory and imagination, as you imagine the maker's process reflected in this object.

This reminds me of Joel Pfeiffer, often considered the forefather of SEC in the US. So much of his work is centered around the act of making clay ("Clay Stomps"), while the finished product (often tile murals) is almost secondary. It's really the connections that are formed through the process and the practices of craft as opposed to the object itself. The object serves as a reminder or a memory or a monument to the actual practice or process.

SHANNON: Let's talk about feminism because so many of these craft practices have been, at some point, gendered. Often, these gendered practices provided meeting places where the conversations about politics and social issues could happen when they couldn't or wouldn't happen in other areas of society. These practices, these moments of production are political or social spaces.

MARY: One of the greatest hegemonic networks of oppression revolves around the idea of gender. There is so much work to be done on both sides of that equation. I think that women, and queer and trans folks making craft that speaks to their positionality, and similarly, men working in fiber, like Hombres Tejedores[7], are really great examples of how there are so many different ways, so many different tactics (to borrow from Chela Sandoval's *Methodology of the Oppressed*)[8], to take down that network from a variety of positionalities: male, female, gender non-conforming, etc.

SHANNON: I loved Sandoval's description of the barriers we put up when we try and separate and give different languages to practices, which is almost what we are trying to do here: separate Craftivism and SEC. When they share so much language, is it worthwhile to separate them rather than just allowing them to coexist in the same space and to use them interchangeably?

MARY: That is such a great question. I don't think the terms are necessarily interchangeable but they share more than they have difference.

The work that you and I both did in our theses was really pointing out this confused history that both of these terms have and really addressing why that exists. One of the really great things that Sandoval brings up that really works for me, in the way that I like to think about practices, is she situates herself in what she calls a, "topography." And instead of thinking about ourselves in isolated fields, we need to think about ourselves in a whole landscape.

This allows us to focus on this situated positionality (Craftivism or SEC) within the topography of craft and understanding that there is a diverse and varied landscape, but it is all connected and accessible to us.

SHANNON: For me, I see the landscape as moments of quietness and increased volume that Craftivism and SEC can embody. Just like any other activist practice, there are moments where you need to be letter writing to your representatives and there are moments where you need to be on that front-line talking to police officers. In SEC and Craftivism, there are those quiet moments and those moments of increased volume. That makes me feel like they are not that separate because they have that varied landscape in themselves.

MARY: Oh, absolutely. Betsy Greer is credited with coining the term "Craftivism,"[9] her work is very much in support of these quiet moments of reflection.

That's something I can really appreciate about Craftivism from the onset, is that it really does embrace that varied landscape of public and private and it moves quite fluidly between them. Most recently, I loved the way that folks who made #Pussyhats for the Pussyhat Projects[10] were able to participate in protests and greater dialogues, often without leaving their homes.

SHANNON: I'm really curious about the use of evaluative tools within Craftivist or SEC practices. Sometimes, folks in the SEA community will say, "If we use evaluative tools, are we then doing what museum educators have been doing?"... as a museum is a program based around art but not considered art itself, offered to the public, and then receives feedback to improve the program based on that feedback.

For SEC or SEA, an artist goes into a community for their own practice and a social practice. I am curious how do you get an evaluative tool that addresses both aspects?

I think we need a combination of lessons from museum education models and community enrichment models to create an evaluative tool that recognizes that SEA and SEC is not solely social work, but is also not solely art or craft.

I've been involved in museum education on and off, and evaluative tools are so necessary to developing those programs, especially with vulnerable communities. I see evaluative tools as another point of engagement. It is an act of conversation.

MARY: An excellent example of this is the work of Carrie Reichardt in the UK. She calls herself an extreme, or renegade Craftivist, amongst other things. Her advocacy for the relief of political prisoners in the US has come with 20-year-long letter writing campaigns and letter writing with the prisoners themselves. It's deeply tied her to personal relationships with these men. Her work, art and activism, is performed through constant communication.

It would be so interesting to put together an evaluative toolkit, for artists, maybe something that is open source, something that is democratic and ever evolving, this toolkit for artists.

SHANNON: That would be really interesting.

MARY: I think we've come at this from a variety of different angles. But why is it important to name Craftivism or SEC? Particularly when so many of the artists (self-identified) working don't identify as craft persons, or necessarily working in craft, and instead identify themselves as artists who work in craft materials.

SHANNON: For me, I see it as a networking game. I think that saying, "This is a Craftivist piece I made, and here's how I'm going to share it," allows you to find that community that is also addressing similar issues and giving that feedback. It's necessary to have that community to understand what other people are doing with their work. We could rarely define a work as "solely craftivist," or "solely SEC," but I think the power of calling it at least one of those things, if not both, allows you to find other people working in similar ways.

It's a social medium and we should treat it as such.

MARY: You and I are both writers looking at these methods, and the act of naming allows us to think critically about a group of works, a movement, or a method. Naming allows us to more fully explore SEC and Craftivism in a cultural context, not just necessarily in the context of making.

In addition, the act of naming is going to be important in combating confused craft histories, as well as the discipline's inferiority complex. It's two-fold. I think that the craft community is quite happy to argue that we are neglected, compared to art and design, in culture. But there is a gendered, classist, racist history in the art versus craft divide. I think that by naming these practices in writing, we have the opportunity to advance craft as a professional field and as an amateur one.

The histories of both Craftivism and SEC have so many roots in amateurism, in funk, in the DIY movement of the '90s. We are really starting to broaden craft's cultural reach into both fine, professional craft and amateur, DIY, Pinterest craft. I think that both ends of that spectrum are increasingly important to the ways that we continue to self-define as a field.

SHANNON: I like the idea of working for the makers and also for the historians. I'm always trying to think a bit from a curatorial perspective, of how do these things fit together or how are they different and that is important in naming, too. In a bit of a selfish way, that is your legacy? Thinking of a legacy also informs your practice beyond how you'll be perceived but how do you proceed with the ethics of engagement? How do you proceed with the aesthetic standards that you wish for yourself or your communities?

MARY: Perhaps it would just be like naming areas on that craft topography. They're not fences, we're not limited by them, but instead we are able to move fluidly between them.

SHANNON: You have so many more options for your craft and for your community to engage with the work. You're not limiting yourself to a single practice, you're allowing yourself to occupy Craftivism, Socially Engaged Craft, traditional craft, art, activism…

MARY: Right. That diversification of practices is a long time coming in the craft field. The diversification of practices, whether it be with activism, social engagement, or with new technologies like rapid prototyping or fabric printing, only serves to benefit the field and really propel us further.

Authors' Note: Looking forward to the future of both SEC and Craftivism, we see a need for flexible, inclusive language… language that critically perceives and reflects on the needs and results of these practices. The use of terms like SEC and Craftivism will allow for greater reflexivity in our field, as will the use of evaluative tools and feedback measures. Continuing in the tradition of exhibitions like *Social Objects, Across the Table, Across the Land, Queer Threads, Spaces of Production,* and *Gestures of Resistance*[11], we're calling for institutions and individuals to invest their time, energy, and funding in projects that respond to a burgeoning social field and the continued need for engaged publics. As activist and political methods of working, the need for increased participation, careful and ethical communication, and the contemporary practices of SEC and craftivism has never been greater. #CraftIsResistance

For other resources on SEC and Craftivism, please consider:

"Craftivism:" A special issue of Utopian Studies 22, no. 2 (2011). Edited by Maria Elena Buszek and Kirsty Robertson.

You can request a copy of Mary Callahan Baumstark's MA thesis, "Craftivist Clay: Activism and Resistance in Contemporary Ceramics," through her website, bonedrybodies.com

You can request a copy of Shannon Hebert Waldman's undergraduate thesis, "Naming Socially Engaged Craft," through her website directdisorder.wordpress.com

Endnotes

1.   Socially Engaged Craft is a general term that refers to socially engaged, or relational, artworks that involve craft practices or objects while Craftivism is a term coined by Betsy Greer in 2001, a portmanteau of "craft" and "activism."

2.   Shannon Hebert Waldman, "Naming Socially Engaged Craft," (Ashville: Warren Wilson College, 2016).

3.   Mary Callahan Baumstark, "Craftivist Clay: Activism and Resistance in Contemporary Ceramics," (Toronto: OCAD University, 2016).

4.   Johanna Hedva, "Sick Woman Theory," Mask Magazine, Jan. 2016.

5.   Claire Bishop, Radical Museology (Walther König, Köln, 2014).

6.   Namita Gupta Wiggers, "Craft Performs," Hand+Made: The Performative Impulse in Art and Craft for the Contemporary Art Museum 2010.

7.   A male-centric knitting collective in Chile. https://www.facebook.com/hombrestejedores/

8.   Chela Sandoval, Methodology of the Oppressed, (University of Minnesota Press, Minneapolis, 2000).

9.   Betsy Greer, ed. Craftivism: The Art of Craft and Activism, (Arsenal Pulp Press, Vancouver, 2014).

10. The Pussyhat Project, Krista Suh and Jayna Zweiman, 2016-17, https://www.pussyhatproject.com.

11. Social Objects, SECC and c3:Initiative, c3:Initiative, 2017.
     Across the Table, Across the Land, curated by Namita Gupta Wiggers and Michael J. Strand, Charlotte Street Foundation, 2016.
     Queer Threads, curated by John Chaich, Leslie Lohman Museum of Gay and Lesbian Art, 2016.
     Gestures of Resistance, curated by Judith Leemann and Shannon Stratton, Museum of Contemporary Craft, 2010.

Embodied Objects:
Agents of Change

Elizabeth Kozlowski

Art has historically been used as an instrument for engagement, commentary and conflict. What was once perhaps, a more subversive practice now lives directly on the surface of every canvas, cup or community project. Intuition and artistic practice lead us beyond standard limitations and into the realm of real social change.

Socially Engaged Craft (SEC) and material exploration serve as guides towards new ways of thinking about objects and their unrealized potential. I believe these ideas are embedded in craft-based production and can evolve into a practice of innovation in the public sector. How we perceive ourselves and others is defined by what we wear, what we make and what we choose to surround ourselves with. Our embodied relationships with objects construct our social realities. These objects are transformed into living history—a physical representation of our collective culture with the power to enact social change.

Contemporary Craft and design disrupt traditional conventions and delve into serious social issues. Participatory projects give birth to objects that are "made collectively as part of activist movements, and are in themselves tools for social change."[1] These projects transform social gatherings into "hubs of collective political thought." Participatory projects provide a bridge between the institution— tasked with serving not only as stewards of the collection, but also the community— and the audience, lending a personal connection to what ends up on display.

Contemporary artist Margarita Cabrera draws from the political, social and personal experience of being from two distinct, yet intimately entwined cultures— Mexico and the United States. Her practice meets at the intersections of contemporary art and indigenous Mexican folk art and craft traditions. These collaborations not only revive traditional craft practices but also provide participants with the opportunity to feel connected to their new communities.

The ongoing community-based project, *Space in Between*, promotes dialogue centered around themes of immigration, cultural identity, and labor practices. The title comes from the Nahuatl Aztec word "Nepantla" which roughly translates into "space in the middle."[2] For Cabrera, this space represents marginalized cultures and their incredible resilience. Desert cacti and flora indigenous to the Southwestern United States are constructed out of border patrol uniforms and planted in traditional Mexican terracotta pots. Yucca and Nopal can be found alongside the most frequently traveled routes of immigration into the United States— the Mexican border along Texas and Arizona. These plant-like soft sculptures question the role of border patrol officers as protagonists in the American landscape. The historical embroidery techniques adopted from Tenango de Doria Hidalgo employ colorful threads sewn into personal stories of immigration.

I became acutely aware of Christy Mason's work as I ran my hand across the surface of Sonic Structure II, on display in "40 under 40: Craft Futures" at the Renwick Gallery of the Smithsonian American Art Museum in 2012. The interactive textile installation is made of hand-woven cotton and copper, and an electronic circuit that measures changes in electro-magnetic frequencies as the cloth is activated. The audible range of changing frequencies is heard through speakers mounted on a wall near the weavings. Mason's practice integrates weaving and sound using both hand and digital Jacquard looms. A digital loom breaks down images into a binary system of zeros and ones, or "pure information" which the loom then translates into physical material. Mason layers information within the weavings using a combination of hand and digital processes that reference the electronic and physical woven structures of sound.[3] What are the design implications of a textile that can react to touch and produce sound? With the ability to capture an audio file and translate it into the visual realm, the possibilities are endless.

Ceramics has a rich political history as both performative objects and surfaces for critique and dialogue. The archetype of the cup provides a space to explore radical ideas. Sarah Archer, art critic, speaks to the positive effects an "unassuming, humble cup of coffee (and the conversations that happen over it)" can have on its user.[4]

California potter Ehren Tool joined the Marines in 1989 and served during the first Gulf War in Iraq. Continuing the rich legacy of studio craft artists educated by the GI Bill, Tool used the funds to attend college and received his MFA from UC Berkeley in 2005. He began making cups and giving them away in 2001, before 9/11. For him, the cup is personal— the perfect scale to talk about war.[5] The use of war iconography (gas masks, plastic guns, even our American Flag) reveals how abstract war is for most of our culture. We have become so desensitized by imagery of war that we make play out if it.[6] Initially his work was autobiographical and now examines our current Middle Eastern occupation and the veterans that come out of contemporary conflicts. Tool brings his 'war stories' to life on the surface of his cups. The work is performative, confrontational and engages its subjects in heartfelt conversation. It forces the user to ask difficult questions about the nature of war and its effects on society.

In early 2015, Fargo potter Michael Strand began a project to mobilize "Cuplomats," or regular citizens from each state to either hand-deliver, or ship, a cup and saucer to their state senator in Washington, D.C. The "Cuplomacy" project called on legislators to "move across the aisle to the table" and share a cup of coffee and a bipartisan conversation towards change. Each package would contain a mismatched cup and saucer, handcrafted by Strand and collaborators Helen Otterson and Peter Atwood, in order to encourage interaction. The only way to create a matching set was to exchange the unrelated items with a member of the opposite party, and in the process receive a gentle reminder of the importance sitting down together towards a common goal. Strand's future Cuplomacy, and his previous projects, are facilitated by the familiar use and exchange of hand-thrown ceramic wares. The artist defines his process as existing between journalism, social science, activism and functional ceramics.[7]

Ehren Tool and Michael Strand paved the way for a recent political act created via our hands... the Democratic Cup Project. As we sat watching the presidential votes being counted, a friend and I poured over a new purchase that had just arrived, a mug decorated with a cartoon of Ruth Bader Ginsburg. A joint effort between David Gordon and Nick Moen, Ginsburg is depicted in Victorian era dress on one side (a huge opera fan) and in her Justice robes on the other. The Democratic Cup is the brainchild of Ayumi Horie and Nick Moen and raises funds for worthy causes through the sale of limited-edition handmade cups designed by a collaborative team of thirty-two nationally recognized ceramic artists and illustrators. Images of activists, politicians, and historical figures, such as Bernie Sanders, bell hooks, and Sojourner Truth, embellish cups and urge people to vote.[8] Humor, intellect, and a range of human emotions are used to harness our collective energy towards inclusivity of all Americans, regardless of race, religion, gender, sexuality, and culture.

The interdependence craft practice has to the characteristics of material affordance (what clay, textiles, and digital technologies help us to achieve) is the greatest starting point for effecting real time, social change. Having spent many late nights and early mornings discussing the handmade and the need for a revolution— I truly believe it is with our hands and minds that we can mobilize innovation for the greater good.

Endnotes

1. Harriet Baker, "Rebellion by Design: When Ceramics and Textiles Get Radical," Financial Times, 8/8/14, https://www.ft.com/content/7612b3bc-18a4-11e4-933e-00144feabdc0
2. Margarita Cabrera, "Space In Between," Margarita Cabrera, 2016, http://www.margaritacabrera.com/portafolio/space-in-between/.
3. Syniva Whitney, "The Grid, Weaving, Body and Mind." Textiles and Settlement: From the Plains Space to Cyber Space, Textile Society of America 12th Biennial Symposium, Lincoln, Nebraska. 10/2010
4. Sarah Archer, "The Democratic Cup," Huffington Post Blog, 10/10/2016, http://www.huffingtonpost.com/sarah-archer/democratic-cup_b_12303138.html
5. Melissa Stern, "Peace and Grief in the Art of US Veterans," Hyperallergic, 2/12/17, http://hyperallergic.com/357541/peace-and-grief-in-the-art-of-us-veterans/
6. Nikki Grattan, "Interview with Ehren Tool," In The Make, 10/2011, http://inthemake.com/Ehren-Tool/
7. Michael J. Strand, "Philosophy," Michael J. Strand, http://www.michaeljstrand.com/#!philosophy
8. The Democratic Cup, "About Us," The Democratic Cup, https://www.thedemocraticcup.com/pages/about-us

The Role of Craft to Reflect and Shape Culture

Lauren Karle

According to Claire Bishop, "[Umberto] Eco regarded the work of art as a *reflection* of the conditions of our existence in a fragmented modern culture, while [Nicholas] Bourriaud sees the work of art *producing* these conditions"[1]. Art has the potential to both reflect our experiences and shape them. As a socially engaged ceramic artist I respond to both of these responsibilities to society. My experiences have shaped my view of craft and socially engaged art. I approach the making of my work knowing that it has the potential to be the interface between people and relationships.

Craft reflects identity. One of the most powerful examples of this is the personal relationship between a person and the garments they wear. I observed this firsthand while living in Guatemala and Mexico. The length of the Mayan huipils, or blouses, convey marital status, the number of panels sewn together reflect a person's economic level, and the pattern is specific to their village. The woven fabrics

relate ancient and modern histories to anyone who is willing to listen. They speak of indigenous peoples concerned with upholding their customs in a contemporary setting. They speak of cultures, and of the image different peoples hold of themselves and of others. They speak of the way of thinking in a part of Mexico where a tradition of creating beauty is a daily practice.[2]

Handmade objects are a reflection of people and place long before the separation of utility from beauty.

Not only do I admire these blouses as symbols of identity and protectors of culture, I feel a deep connection with fellow crafts-women who spend hours stitching them by hand. I layer the surfaces of each ceramic object I make with meaningful pattern, imbuing my work with identity, culture, and my environment. I believe in the power of craft to communicate our human condition far into the future.

Craftsmanship does not last forever, but it is not disposable. "It follows the course of time from day to day, flowing along with us, gradually wearing out, neither pursuing death nor denying it, but rather, accepting it. The craft object teaches us to die, and by doing so, teaches us to live".[3]

Mexican Talavera, a traditional form of pottery brought over from Talavera de la Reina, Spain during colonization, is a mixture of Islamic, Italian, Spanish, and Mexican ceramic techniques. Designs of Islamic pottery were brought to Spain by the Moors as Hispano-Moresque ware at the end of the 12th century. This style continued to influence the rest of Spain and Europe and were brought to Puebla during the early colonial period. The lines between what is local and what has originated in other cultures are blurred. The influence of multiple cultures extend as an export good by entering people's lives around the world. For example, Talavera tiles adorn a fountain and façade of a shopping mall in Kansas City, Missouri, bringing a part of their culture and history to the United States. The fountain illustrates how craft can unify many traditions through time, cross political boundaries, and bring one culture to another.[4]

Likewise, I am constantly learning to understand my own diverse cultural personal experiences. My passion for the people and culture of Latin America form a hybrid with my native culture that secures a sense of self and belonging in a transcultural society. Just as Talavera artists build on traditions of the past, I seek to unify my different cultural experiences through visually layering meaning and carefully considering how my work enters the world.

It is not only the maker who contributes to the meaning of the objects. As pots are used, meals are served on them, experiences and memories surrounding the objects grow. This was apparent when I attended Utilitarian Clay in 2012. Presenters were asked to talk about their favorite pot. As they caressed the pot in their hands, some had tears fall as they described the people they shared a meal with over it. It was not the beauty of the object but the memories embedded within that made it valuable. After much discussion about the economic challenges of a potter, I left with my heart full knowing that this is why I choose to be an artist. There is power in the use of an object.

I began to think about situating my objects in the world in order to facilitate community. By joining and darting slabs, I build utilitarian forms inherently linked to the history of food and beverages. Sharing life-giving sustenance is one of the most intimate and universal acts, often a catalyst between people and relationships. I see my objects as facilitators to strengthen community connections, aid in cultural sharing, and promote social interaction. Through shared experiences, such as eating a meal together or sipping tea, people can find commonalities amongst their unique backgrounds.

Socially engaged art is by no means new, but recognition as an art genre began in the late 1900s. Rooted in both the arts and sciences, it is changing how we define visual culture and the role of art as a tool for social and environmental change. SEA combines aspects of research, social interaction, performance, and aesthetics to generate projects that create fervent social changes.

Since socially engaged art is relatively new in academia and reaches across many disciplines, I ran into challenges as a MFA candidate. My work inherently involves communities and people. Since these actions or projects are considered "research" by the College of Arts and Sciences at Kansas State University, I was asked to go through the International Review Board process. As Sarah McNutt and

I stated in *Public Art Practice,*

> *The International Review Board (IRB) was set up to protect human subjects during scientific research. In writing an IRB proposal the researcher is forced to structure his or her entire research, which in the case of public art practice, is outlining an entire event. This does not allow for interactions to evolve organically, and an IRB can hinder the art that happens in conversation. It could even be viewed as infringing on freedom of expression. At the same time, artists often try to compare themselves to scientists, arguing that what they do is research. The research an artist does contributes to the world just like a scientist does, however the practical application and modes of demonstrating this research are very different. An artist's creative activity demands a certain amount of freedom from the restrictions of IRBs. This leaves us stuck between the desire for equality with the sciences, and the need to break from the restrictions of the scientific process of human research.[5]*

After reflecting on these projects, I'm aware of how I need to try to engage communities. Working with communities takes time and trust, something that unfolds slowly over time, with the right circumstances. An event or project must consider all perspectives and people involved. In order to ensure an ethical and genuine engagement, what is given and taken must be an equal exchange. Although my biggest motivation in life is to build community and authentic connections, it is my largest fear to ignorantly insult or unknowingly take advantage of people. There are potential negative implications inherent in social art, if it is not done in a highly sensitive fashion. With patience and awareness I believe that the rewards are worthwhile for myself and others.

Art and handicrafts have the capacity to unite people, preserve culture, help us understand each other, and safe-guard the beauty of history. I strive to touch the lives of as many people as possible through my craft, community, and passion for humanity.

Endnotes
1. Claire Bishop, "Antagonism and Relational Aesthetics," <u>October,</u> 2000: 60.
2. Margarita Orellana, "A Weft of Voices,"in T<u>he Crafts of Mexico. Artes de Mexico,</u> (Smithsonian Books, United States of America,2004): 196.
3. Octavio Paz, "Seeing and Using: Art and Craftsmanship," in <u>The Crafts of Mexico. Artes de Mexico,</u> (Smithsonian Books, United States of America,2004): 23.
4. Lauren Karle, "The Talavera Tradition at Uriarte," <u>Ceramics Monthly,</u> June 2014: 24-28.
5. Lauren Karle and Sarah McNutt. "Public Art Practice," <u>Ceramics Technical,</u> Fall 2015 No.41: 94-99.

On Practice

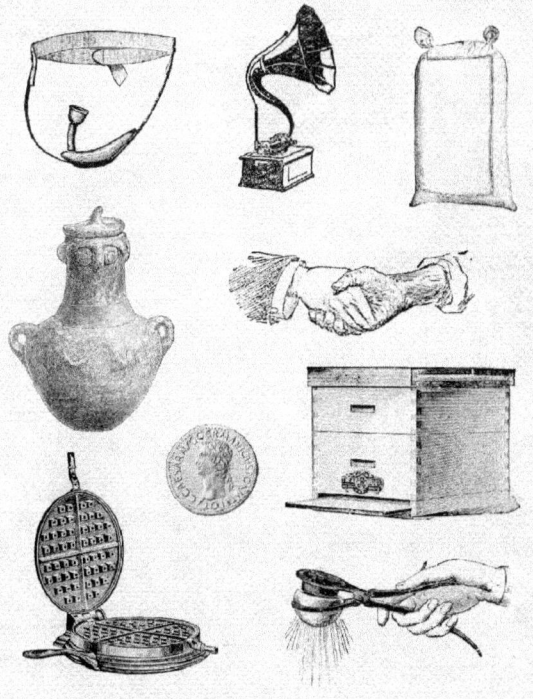

Projects, stories, working definitions, essays and interviews
by members of the Socially Engaged Craft Collective

Backpack/Kiln

Henry James Haver Crissman

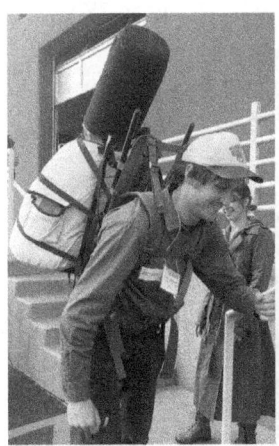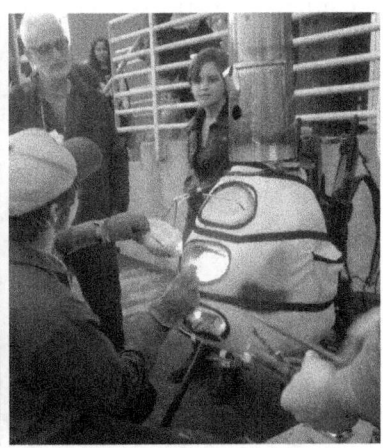

I constructed Backpack/Kiln in the spring of 2016 for a project I won't tell you about right now. Upon its completion, the kiln's maiden firing was held as the event 'Something S'more' which occurred as part of the opening reception festivities of the 'Across the Table, Across the Land' exhibition that was curated by Michael Strand and Namita Gupta Wiggers for the 50th Annual NCECA Conference in Kansas City, MO. 'Something S'more' looked at the opening reception as an opportunity to prop up the content of the exhibition, which was a survey of artists' projects from the year prior that had used pairings of ceramics and food as vehicles for social engagement. Prompts regarding overarching themes and questions of the exhibition were presented along with images and artifacts from the showcased events. 'Something S'more' served as an example of concepts presented, creating both the opportunity experience them and a space to discuss them further.

An analog speaker/cup with commemorative imagery detailing the event was the only object fired in the kiln during the event, and the entire event was recorded on an old iPhone. Following the firing, the iPhone now plays the recording through the speaker (when its not being used as a cup). As such, the object now presents the story of its production, the critical discussion of itself, and the event it supported, and in this way, it quite literally asks for a reconsideration of how we might assess the value of objects.

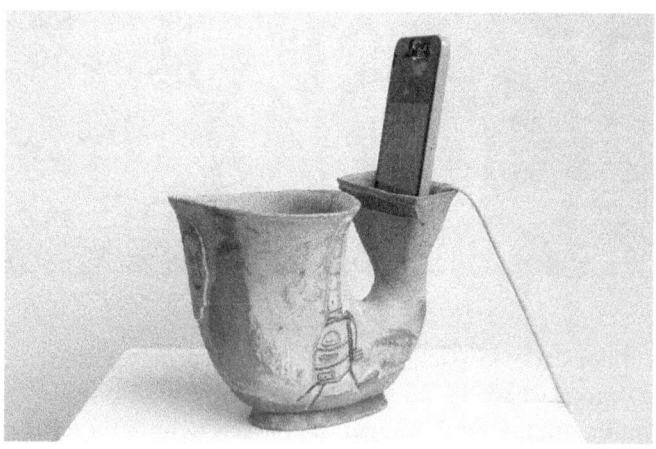

A journal entry intended to be published in the Social Objects publication

Today is January 20th, 2017. It is the due date for entries to this Social Objects publication, and more pressingly, it is the day of the inauguration of a new president who has clearly expressed a complete inability to empathize. Empathy is defined by Google as, "the ability to understand and share the feelings of another." From an evolutionary perspective, it seems that being able to empathize functions to inspire us to do what is best for the collective society, and not just what is best for ourselves.

Art is defined by Google as, "the expression or application of human creative skill and imagination..." Without empathy, making art would be a pointless affair. The capacity to express would be lost by the inability to receive. Without art, attempts to connect to others would be limited to statements of truths and lies. As facts no longer seem to influence opinion, it seems all too sensible that our new authoritarian leader has stated plans to cut funding to the National Endowment for the Arts, the government institution which enables cross cultural connections that serve to unify and empower our fractured citizenry. This move terrifies me for its sinister logic, deeply saddens me in considering what might be its repercussions, and reaffirms to me why the arts are so important.

Despite the measurable economic returns, centuries of people in all cultures across the globe have exposed the true value of art as its ability perpetuate empathetic tendencies. The very tendencies that Trump aims to discourage. Tendencies to bring people together. Tendencies to resist complacency. Tendencies to expose injustice and call others to action. Tendencies that may in turn operate on a personal and yet equally profound scale, to expose the reality of oneself to oneself.

As I sit with this privilege to consider myself and the connections I may be able to make via my art, via this essay, etc, it's easy to be overwhelmed by feelings for the immensity of the issues at hand, and doubts regarding the impact of what I can do.

Walking through the Detroit Institute of Arts this afternoon with one of my students, he asked me if I thought about sustainability in my art. I began to answer by talking about ecological sustainability, and then sustainability with regard to how an artist sustains their practice, and then we were stopped by the most stunning fourth century Iranian earthenware platter, intricately decorated with the most luscious pattern of blue, green, yellow, brown and white glazes. We stopped talking and looked at the plate. And then we agreed that all we can ever do is continue to try our best, whatever and wherever that might be.

Experiments in Menstrual Taboos and Stigma

Mary Callahan Baumstark

My experimental project, The Menstrual Cup Project, will speak to the social taboo and stigma of menstruation, and attempt to dissolve some of that with discussion, a few drinks, and handmade objects. This project consists of cast, ceramic menstrual cups - a hygienic, silicone menstruation product that is a sustainable, reusable, and safe - each decorated, on the outside, with facts about menstruation, access to menstrual care, and information about the stigma, taboo, and harmful practices directed towards menstruators.

I'll carry these ceramic menstrual cups on a tray, like a cocktail waitress, and I'll fill each menstrual cup with shot of a cocktail (or mocktail, if you prefer). Yes, the beverage is red... this is not censored advertising with a mysterious, blue liquid poured over a pad or tampon.

Participants will donate funds in exchange for a menstrual cup (to keep) and a shot. These funds benefit Transition Projects in Portland, a non-profit which will use the proceeds to support women facing homelessness, including providing menstrual supplies. By combining the ideas of "souvenir" and "shot glass" in one, the menstrual cups are meant to evoke a fun, casual setting to discuss an awkward, socially taboo topic, and provide participants with an object to recall the experience.

So you might buy a menstrual cup shot for you and your friend, knock it back, and, with a flush in your cheeks, say to the person next to you, "Hey, did you know menstruation occurs in primates, such as apes and monkeys, as well as bats and the elephant shrew?!"

Or, "Not all menstruators are women. Trans men, intersex folks, and gender nonbinary people menstruate, too."

The Menstrual Cup Project engages participants with handmade, ceramic shot glasses and asks them to consider the stigma of menstruation within a silly, celebratory experience. This project is not large, national, or far-reaching. It's a local conversation on a specific topic which results in do-good fundraising, thoughtful conversation, and a little nervous laughter.

Living With Death As An Object

Amanda Leigh Evans

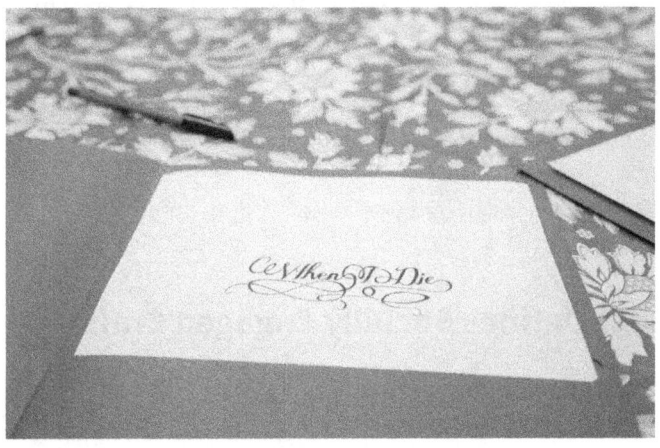

From and To Dust is an ongoing ceramic urn project created with people in the greater Portland area. The project is built through 1-on-1 collaborative relationships to design and produce a personalized cremation urn. Project participants include Mortuary Science community college students, senior citizens, and younger people who have terminal illnesses. Through a collaborative design process, participants and I work together create their own urn, which ultimately becomes a complex and abstracted self-portrait of its maker/user. When the urn is complete, it then lives in the home of its owner until someday it is used for its intended purpose.

The urns are intertwined with another public project I produced in 2016 called *When I Die*, a will writing workshop where people draft, discuss, witness and sign their own legal will. While a typical will designates to whom valuables are given, this modified will template diverges from that format into a poetic, functional document-as-artwork. The *When I Die* document holds space for participants to share who they are, how they intend to live their lives, the legacy they want to leave behind, and the people who inherit the objects they treasure most. At the end of the workshop, participants witness and sign each other's wills, rendering them legally valid.

If you would like to download your own *When I Die* will template, visit my website. Find two witnesses to sign it and you have your own valid, legal will.

www.amandaleighevans.com/When-I-Die

What Defines Socially Engaged Craft?

In the fall of 2010, I was introduced to Socially Engaged Art through a social object. I was studying abroad in New York City with my friend Monica Tzeng, who was lucky enough to get one of the keys from Paul Ramirez Jonas' *Key to the City* project. She stood in a long line at Times Square until she reached a platform where the person ahead of her read some official words, shook her hand, and ceremoniously presented her with a gold key and small passport booklet. By the time the other students and I learned of the project, the keys were all gone, so we shared Monica's key amongst us. This treasured object gave us the opportunity to discover the city together by visiting sites that otherwise would have been invisible to us. That fall, I felt as though the city had been passed along to me by artists who had come before me, and when I left I passed it along to the young artists who were arriving. One small social object opened the door to the endless secrets and possibilities of a new city.

The *Key to the City* has influenced how I think about objects as catalysts in social experiences. The power of an object centers around its function and activation. Although I have fallen in love with many art and craft objects on pedestals throughout my life, ultimately I am not satisfied by making work that remains in that state. I want my work to continue to have an active life when it leaves my hands, not to live in a storage archive after an exhibition (a phenomenon was once described to me by my mentor Christopher Miles as "the sculptor's dilemma"). When I make objects, I want them to be lived with and to be used.

Craft has been taught, learned and passed along through embodied knowledge by everyday people for millennia. It is the amalgamation of techniques, styles, and practices of vernacular cultures and self-organized communities of unknown craftspeople. Socially Engaged Craft can engage this history by emphasizing the social meaning of handmade objects, questioning the value of craft labor in an era of mass production, and creating space for more people to make objects by hand. Ultimately for me, Socially Engaged Craft is a space to process why I am am maker and explore the questions that sustain my practice. Who gets to be an artist? Whose histories inform our knowledge and practice? Who is the audience for contemporary art and craft objects? What is the economy of this work? How do we build a more accessible clay community?

Socially Engaged Craft: A Potter's Approach

Jeni Hansen Gard

As a socially engaged craft artist, I use the ceramic vessel to explore our ecological relationship with plants as food through growing, cooking, eating, and sharing meals. Using craft as a premise, my work draws on a critical under-standing of human relationships and the merger between art and life. I design civic projects that focus on the meal, personal food choices, food as a form of communication, and the ceramic vessel as a transmitter and artifact. Using an object-based process in the ceramic arts, and a commu-nity-based, socially engaged art practice I make functional objects intended for use in everyday life and orchestrate the parameters surrounding their use by engaging participants. This human involvement is what distinguishes my work from traditional pottery and brings it into the sphere of socially engaged craft.

My studio work is a consideration of form, function, pattern, and color of the ceramic vessel. My work exists as physical objects as well as social projects in which the vessel serves as a catalyst in creating a food dialogue. I am attempt-ing to turn viewers into active participants by inviting them to become users, and thus extending the value of the individual object outward toward the community. The indi-vidualized design of these handmade objects, even within sets, is a way to focus people on a specific experience and to create mindfulness in eating. There is value added in both the aesthetic of handmade dishes, the experience of eating in this format, and the benefits visually, socially, and nutritionally of making certain choices. Through use, the vessel has the ability to elevate the food we consume and asks the viewers to reconsider what they eat, who they eat with, what they eat from, and how food affects our bodies. After use the vessel remains imprinted in our memory as a carrier of stories. Even after use, the vessel remains as an artifact and carrier of memory and story.

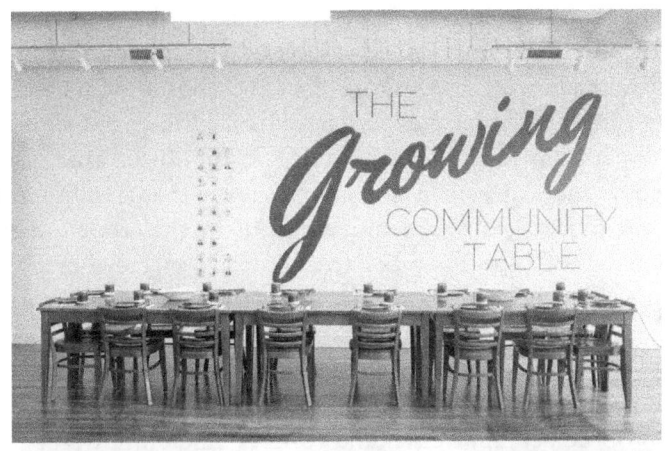

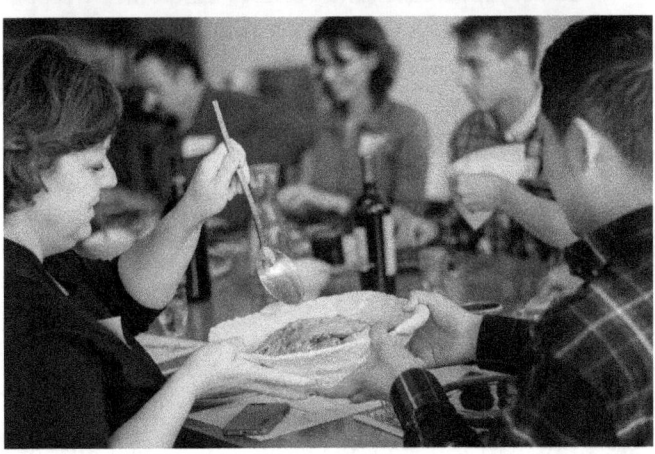

What Defines Socially Engaged Craft?

Objects carry stories. Often we look at the past story of objects, analyzing and interpreting to create meaning. Looking at the history of art-as-social-engagement, I found relational-based art, as in Relational Aesthetics, Social Practice, and Socially Engaged Art. In all of these practices, the objects are often looked over in lieu of focusing on art as the experience. For example, Rirkrit Tiravanija in his work *Untitled (Free)* used the gallery as a place to gather and eat, serving rice and curry to anyone who visited.[1] He created art through the audience's interaction, using the audience as a medium. Tiravanija provided tables, chairs, and disposable dishware allowing the visitors to sit and engage with each other in a shared meal experience. Socially Engaged Craft emerged from these fields with a focus on objects that support the experience and an experience that is supported by the object. Objects are usually made by the artist to meet the needs of a specific project. As a socially engaged craft maker I look to help construct a very personal future story together with people using handmade ceramic vessels.

My approach to Socially Engaged Craft is rooted in historical pottery, with a focus on the aesthetics and function of the ceramic vessel. The vessel is inherently wrapped in the social sphere of human interaction. As a potter, there is a natural connection to people and food as one makes objects for daily use. The carryover from traditional pottery to relational-based art becomes clear here, as potters have created relational objects long before the appearance of Relational Aesthetics. There is an extensive history of crafts addressing the needs of society through the creation of vessels. In Socially Engaged Craft, we design and consider the surface and content of the vessel to convey a message that is not possible with mass-produced dishware. The dishes exist as a relational device of connectivity.

Nicolas Bourriaud, in his book, *Relational Aesthetics*, suggested that art can exist as a catalyst in human relationships. Bourriaud defines relational art as something that evolves around "the whole of human relations and their social context"[3]. Claire Bishop gives a counterargument to relational art, as she questions the focus on the "relationship between (people) rather than the object itself"[3]. Socially Engaged Craft differs from both Bourriaud's or Bishop's definition of Relational Art in that Socially Engaged Craft revolves around an object to be used and contemplated.

While presenting at Open Engagement 2016, we discussed that Socially Engaged Craft uses crafted objects (or materials) to support social engagement. This contemporary practice is rooted in the history of the craft object as a social object in society. Socially Engaged Craft applies this object-focused practice to the more contemporary movements of Relational Aesthetics, Social Practice, and Socially Engaged Art. By using objects to help facilitate, personalize, direct attention or focus, and further social engagement. Socially Engaged Craft artists see objects and experience to be of equal importance.[4]

Little scholarly writing exists on the coined term Socially Engaged Craft so my research has looked broadly to relational-based art. Author and critic Claire Bishop says, "by using people as a medium, participatory art has always had a double ontological status: it is both an event in the world, and also at a remove from it. As such, it has the capacity to communicate on two levels to participants and to spectators"[5]. Socially Engaged Craft is capable of the same. In *Living as Form*, Anne Pasternak remarks "artists create forms of living that activate communities and advance public awareness of pressing social issues"[6]. The non-discipline specific nature of the projects covered in *Living as Form* help to illustrate the difference between Socially Engaged Craft and Socially Engaged Art. At the same time, the underlying themes are consistent people, relationships, engagement, interaction, and the ability to go beyond gallery walls. The emphasis on participation over object is what distinguishes them.

As an advocate for Socially Engaged Craft and a member of the Socially Engaged Craft Collective I hope to help challenge the western canon, support its inclusion in education, and promote diversification and growth in the field. It is important as educators, curators, writers, and artists that we make room at the table for Socially Engaged Craft.

Endnotes

1. Rirkrit Tiravanija, Untitled (Free). New York. NY: 303 Gallery (1992) & David Zwirner Gallery (2007).
2. Nicolas Bourriaud, Relational Aesthetics, (S. Pleasance & F. Woods, Trans.). Dijon, France: Les Presses Du Reel. (Original work published in 1998), 113. Nicolas Bourriaud, Relational Aesthetics, in C. Bishop (Ed.), Participation, (London: The MIT Press), 160.
3. Claire Bishop, "Antagonism and Relational Aesthetics," October, 2000: 51-79.
4. Jeni Hansen Gard of the Socially Engaged Craft Collective, "The power of the object," presented at the meeting of Open Engagement (Oakland, April, 2016).
5. Claire Bishop, "Participation and spectacle: Where are we now?" presented at Living as form: Socially Engaged Art from 1991- 2011 (New York, May 2011).
6. Anne Pasternak, in N. Thompson (Ed.) Living as form: Socially Engaged Art from 1991-2011 (The MIT Press, Cambridge, MA, 2012): 8.

Waffle Toss:
A Game for the Kitchen

Forrest Sincoff Gard

Waffle Toss: A Game for the Kitchen is an interactive installation for the gallery inspired by a common household object, the toaster. In this participatory game, participants attempt to toss a ceramic waffle into a foam toaster, and select and keep a Golden-Syrup trophy waffle as a prize.

I used a number of different craft materials and processes in the creation of this project. I "drew" a waffle three-dimensionally using a CAD program and had it 3-D printed. This process allowed me to design and make extra large waffles, so after shrinking from the drying and firing processes, the waffles would be the size of a real frozen waffle. Next, I made a mother mold, which was used to make numerous plaster working molds. I colored hundreds of clay balls with ceramic stains, hand pressed the balls into waffles, and then fired the waffles in a kiln to cone 6 (2232 F). My intention was not to make the waffles look so real that the audience is tricked, but rather to make them look realistic enough so that people are comfortable picking them up and playing with them. I have found engagement is less likely to happen if the waffles look like porcelain and if they are far too small they appear to look more like a toy.

I sculpted the toaster in plaster first, which allowed me to make larger-than-normal slots. After that, I made another mold and cast a soft, foam toaster. In an effort to increase participation, I exaggerated the size of the toaster slots. This gives participants the perception that the game is easy, or at least possible, kind of like a carnival game! I designed a faux-counter-top and three trophy shelves specifically for this project. These were built out of wood and painted white, to directly reference to the color traditionally used in galleries and museums.

By crafting the objects as well as the displays, I can determine every detail, such as the dimensions, forms, colors, and textures, making the best decisions possible for maximum engagement. At the first Waffle Toss event, over 60 people engaged directly by playing the game and several

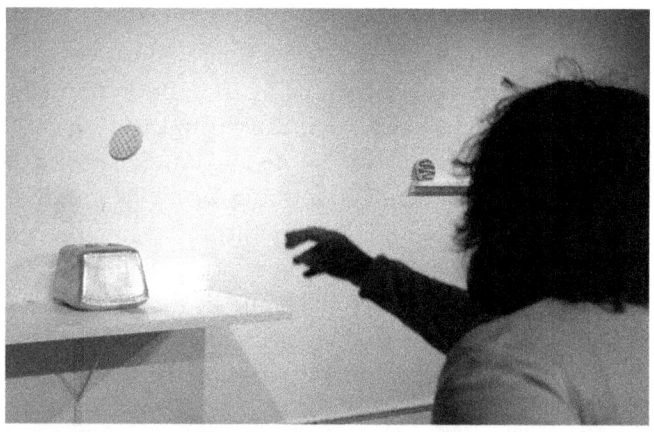

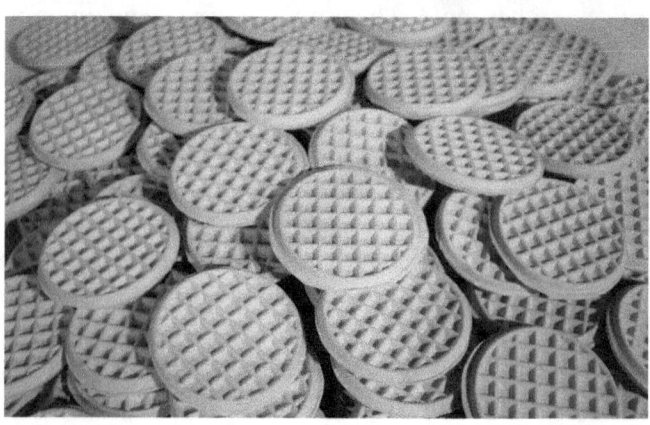

hundred engaged indirectly as spectators who cheered and celebrated. It was exciting to observe the wide range of human emotion that happened as result of the socially engaged piece: excitement, joy, fear, risk, disbelief, awe, and a dozen different celebration dances!

Two Unknown Influences of Socially Engaged Craft

My interest in Socially Engaged Craft grew from my appreciation for handmade objects during my formal training in ceramics and my interest in Interactive Art. As an artist, I was drawn away from the pedestal and started to make ceramic objects that engaged the audience by allowing them to touch and play games in the gallery.

I think of Socially Engaged Craft (SEC) as art or an art project that uses a crafted object (or craft material) to engage people, and through their engagement the artwork is completed. There are many interactive, performance, activist, time-based, and installation artworks that are considered socially engaged craft. Here are two artists I would like to acknowledge who are lesser known for their impact on Socially Engaged Art, and ultimately on Socially Engaged Craft: Marcel Duchamp and Myron Krueger.

Marcel Duchamp is well known for his "Readymades" (such as *Fountain,* 1917). Despite his fame, Duchamp does not immediately come to mind as one of the first artists to create an artwork for the gallery that was completed through social engagement. In 1920, Duchamp exhibited his *Rotary Glass Plates*, a kinetic art piece and optical illusion that only worked while spinning. Accompanying the art piece were instructions, which told the viewer to, "Turn on the machine and stand at a distance of one meter."[1] Without the viewer plugging in the machine, the piece would remain still and the illusion would not function properly. It was up to the viewer to follow instructions and plug in the machine. Only then, with their engagement, was the artwork completed. Later Duchamp famously claimed that "The creative act is not performed by the artist alone; the spectator brings the work in contact with the external world by deciphering and interpreting its inner qualification and thus adds his contribution to the creative act."[2]

Myron Krueger's *Responsive Environments* were highly interactive artworks and focused primarily on social engagement. The first of these responsive environments, in 1969, was *GlowFlow*, a darkened room with lines of glowing light on the wall. The light was made possible by pumping phosphorescent particles through tubes that passed through columns, revealing the light. In front of each column was a pressure sensitive pad that reacts to footsteps. The reaction of the footsteps allowed the computer to respond by changing the lighting or changing sounds, creating a direct interaction between the person, computer, and the environment. *Glow-Flow* led Krueger to make a number of valuable conclusions about Socially Engaged Art, which he referred to as Interactive Art. Krueger believed that "the visual response should not be judged as art nor the sounds as music. The only aesthetic concern is the quality of the interaction."[3]

I consider people to be crucial components and actors in my work. Combined with ceramic objects, it is only with their presence and interaction along with their feelings, experiences, and emotional reactions am I successful in creating Socially Engaged Craft.

Endnotes

1. Robert Lebel, *Marcel Duchamp* (New York: Paragraphic Books, 1959) 77,78
2. Christian Paul, *Digital Art* (London: Thames and Hudson, 2008), 5
3. Myron Krueger, *Responsive Environments,* Montvale, New Jersey, AFIPS Press, 1977

awe/agency

nicole gugliotti

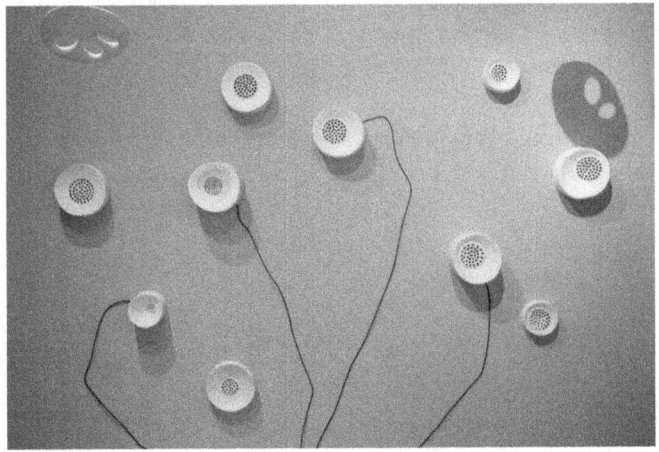

awe/agency is an art project that seeks to change the dominant narrative and challenge stigma surrounding abortion in the United States. People who have had abortions are at worst, cast as villains, at best, as victims, and rarely as heroes of their own story. This project combines individual stories with installation art and sculpture both in the gallery and as an online resource.

By interviewing people who have had an abortion and self-identify this experience as positive, I hope to offer an alternative narrative. Inspiration for this project came when a close friend sharing her abortion experience with me. I was aware of this distinct lack of shame that she modeled. Her experience was not without hesitation but it came from a place of knowing she was entitled to her decision and her humanity. After that I went searching and found several young folks who have chosen to talk about their abortion experience on YouTube. The motivation for each differs but often folks share their experiences in order to dispel fear, myths or other misunderstandings for others. These stories are told in a way that is factual, clear and free from persuasion.

How would access to reproductive healthcare look if that were the norm instead of the exception?

For myriad reasons, choosing to have an abortion may be difficult. However, societal pressure, stigma and stereotype shouldn't be the driving force in how one's goes about difficult decisions.

By telling their stories, the people in my project offer an alternative to the dominant narrative. They can offer us a model for how making informed, empowered and stigma-free healthcare decisions could be.

Touch in Real Time

Holly Hanessian

I work in the realm of the senses and in particular, the sense of touch. My work in the exhibition Social Objects dives below the surface in an interactive participatory action different from my earlier work.

This year I am exhibiting the project "Touch in Real Time" created between 2012-2015 in two shows, "Crooked Data: (Mis)Information in Contemporary Art" at the Joel and Lila Harnett Museum of Art in Richmond, Virginia and in Cont[ract] Earth, and the First Central China Biennale at the Henan Museum in Zhengzhou, China curated by Wendy Gers. The artworks on exhibit show hundreds of porcelain handshakes made from performances that took place in twelve states in the USA and in China with over 2000 people.

Two people would hold hands with a wet piece of clay between there them for two-five minutes creating both a human bond and an imprint from both hands. These clay pieces were later fired in a kiln and became an artifact of the moment. Additionally, the moment of bonding often resulted in the release of oxytocin, a hormone that may initiate a connection of human warmth to one another.

In the show, the "Artifact of Touch" taking place in China, the artifacts are shown along with ancient Chinese ceramic shards with new handshakes made from local clay

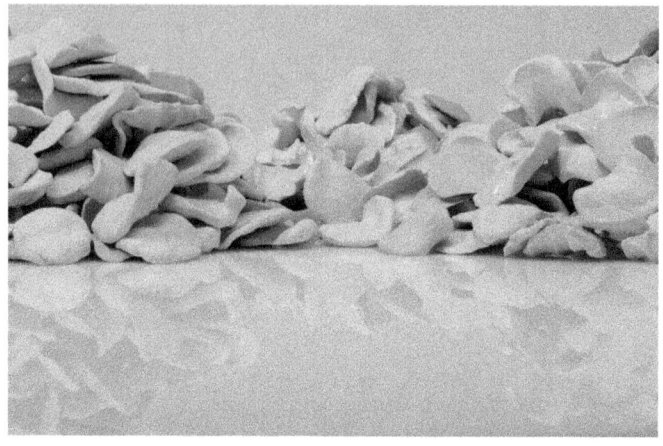

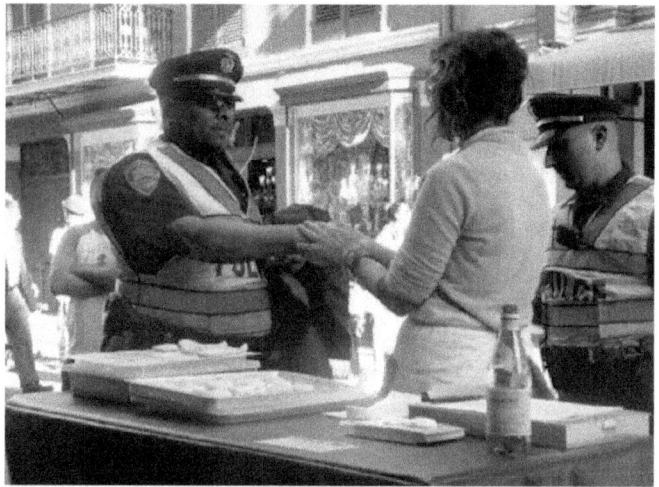

and the surrounding community of people who live or visited the Henan Museum in an installation. All of the artifacts represent a continuum of ceramics acting as a bridge from the past to the present. Each piece, whether old or new symbolizes the power of touch, the human thread connecting us as a global culture and acting as unifying bridge to the longevity of human activity of ceramics on the earth.

What Defines Socially Engaged Craft?

I remember putting a piece of wet clay into a policeman's hand during one of my Touch in Real Time performances in New Orleans in the French Quarter. His mirrored glasses, impermeable helmet, and large black hand covered mine and as we held hands, I realized how anxious I was. Breathing deeply, I wanted to connect and be able to move beyond our race, gender, and social standing. My hope, and it's a rather big one, is that our touch through clay made this barrier breakdown. Realistically, it may not, but he may always remember that moment and I now have that fired porcelain handshake as a reminder.

As I reflect on my definition of a "Socially Engaged Art Practice," I believe the idea of creating this type of artwork examines or makes the audience aware of basic core injustices by looking deeply at the divide that exists in our culture. We, the artists, want to empower and bring a mirror to those who are disenfranchised through an art related or human-to-human craft activist experience. The use of craft-based materials that we conscientiously weave into our artwork reflect back on craft's long history of serving culture and acting as a conduit for an accessible human connection.

Weaving Dialogues

Lauren Karle and Jeni Hansen Gard

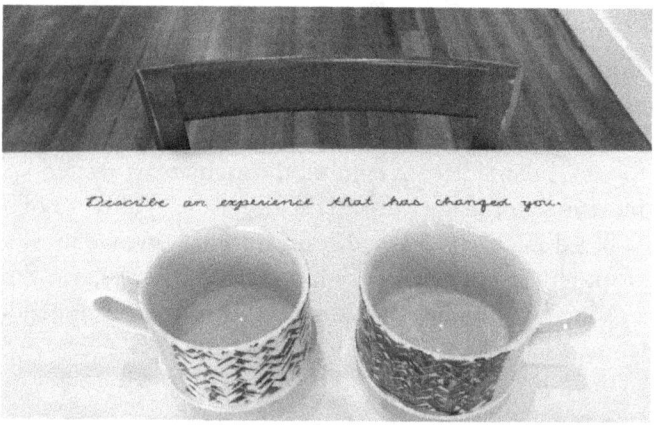

The goals of our project, Weaving Dialogues, are to allow people to connect with other people through shared conversation and to experience handmade objects. We collaboratively made pairs of mugs using porcelain clay. The surfaces are inspired by baskets, which were widely used before ceramics and often influenced early pottery. Basketry is something all cultures around the world have used through time, a symbol of reaching back to our commonalities. The mugs combine our respective skills—Jeni threw small bowl shapes for the bottom to which Lauren attached slabs and handles.

Before the first event, we hand embroidered each tablecloth with the starting prompt, "Describe an experience that has changed you." When all guests arrived we set the expectations for the experience by talking about how important community is, how we should approach others with curiosity, and embrace differences as learning opportunities. Participants were paired up with someone they did not already know. Each pair chose a matching set of mugs from their respective table and were offered hot coffee or tea. The first event took place at Denison Art Space in Newark, Ohio and began with the prompt posed by us. At the end of the session participants were asked to leave a statement where their conversation left off. Future iterations will take place across the country including Portland, Oregon, and Las Vegas, New Mexico. These will build on the previous prompt, symbolically creating one dialogue between all participants. The words embroidered on the tablecloth provide a glimpse into the conversations that took place at each table, leaving future viewers to ponder what was said between the questions.

Weaving Dialogues varies as it travels to different locations in an effort to meet the needs of that community and/or hosting organization. At the Denison Art Space we focused on connecting residents of the geographically close but disparate communities of Newark and Granville. As the project evolved we realized that the tablecloth became a central component as participants immediately went around reading the prompts and labored over the words to leave behind. Through their handwritten text that we embroider into the cloth and the less planned stains that now cover the top of the white sheets, participants record their history. The tablecloths serve as a way to document the events, weaving thoughts together into a continuous dialogue.

Pop Up Pollinator Picnic

Anna Metcalfe

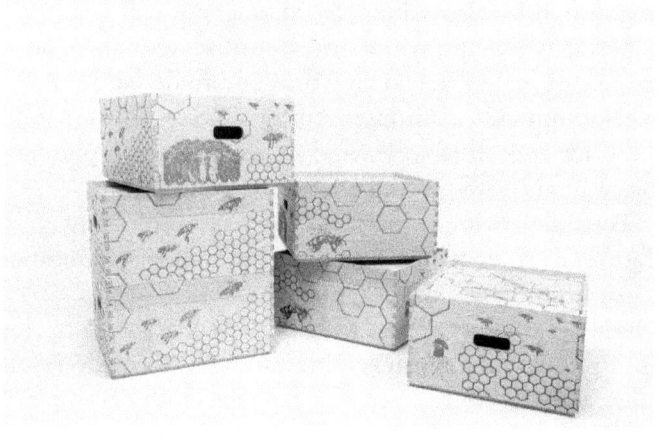

Pop Up Pollinator Picnic engages the urban public in a conversation about the amazing story of the honey bee and its critical relationship to our food systems through public picnics that take place in local urban farms, community gardens and parks. A set of porcelain plates (city map), bowls (hives) and cups (bee-pollinated vegetables) packaged carefully into portable crates and transported on a tricycle are the objects that form a map of the local food system in Minneapolis. The set is a giant puzzle, and participants engage with each other, implementing their collective knowledge of neighborhoods, gardens and beehives to identify the spaces in our city where humans and pollinators mingle. While the conversation is directly about bees and how they intersect with human ecosystems through pollination, talk often turns to other aspects of our food system: farming, food deserts, poverty, race, etc.

I think of bees and beehives as being a metaphor for human communities. Scientists think of a hive as a single organism – individual bees are engaged in a common pursuit to keep the hive healthy and each bee has a role in the system. Communities work in the same way: if some of us are consistently under-served, the entire system will struggle to stay healthy. Bees can teach us the power of interdependence and collaboration. Pop Up Picnic gives community members a chance to discover their role in the food system by interacting with craft objects and food in outdoor spaces.

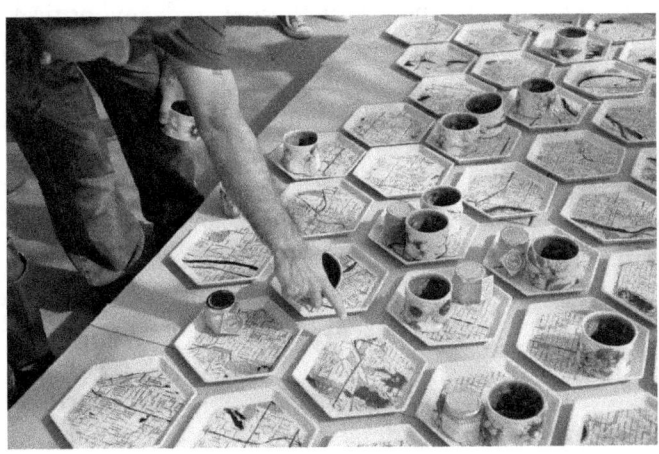

What Defines Socially Engaged Craft?

Socially Engaged Craft places equal value on object and relationship. It attends to both the aesthetics of craft and the aesthetics of engagement. Implicit in the term Socially Engaged Craft is an understanding that craft mediums have always been social - objects are made for common use in a household, passed from generation to generation, or even collectively constructed. Despite the inherently social nature of craft, this is an intentional practice, and collaboration, engagement and conversation are central to its definition.

Craft refers to both the medium and the practice of making. Socially Engaged Craft assumes that value is demonstrated through the deftness of practiced hands on materials that have been used to fashion objects for centuries and that value can be generated from within the object itself through use and context. Socially Engaged Craft artists find themselves heirs to generations of makers in many mediums and we reference, embody and re-invent those traditions and histories.

Socially Engaged Craft recognizes that facilitating empathetic human connection is among the highest forms of making meaning that an artist employs. The aesthetics of engagement are honed through time, study and critical theory. It values acceptance, listening and compassion in all encounters, whether they last for 10 seconds or 10 years.

Socially Engaged Craft circumvents hierarchies reinforced in the arts and in society by promoting inclusivity through direct audience participation and by welcoming traditional ways of working with materials, especially those commonly practiced by women, indigenous peoples and communities of color. It rejects a culture of speed: fast-food, get rich quick, and hasty decisions. Instead, it recognizes that the collaborative process requires time and it honors the slow, deliberate process of making objects and forming relationships. It crosses boundaries, real and imagined, and encourages audiences to do the same.

The Lemon-Aider

Cheyenne Rudolph

The Lemon-Aider is an interactive beverage cart, designed as a traveling performance piece to challenge the collective assumptions surrounding gender identity and self-sacrifice of women. A nostalgic lemonade stand, the Lemon-Aider is operated by a caricatured female. Her good intentions in service are peppered with indecorous insinuations brought on by the mechanics of operating the juicing device. This is not your childhood lemonade stand.

To begin, the Lemon-Aider arrests the viewer with its overstated retro aesthetic, pastel colors, and cartoonish proportions. The viewer is greeted by weighty sacks of fragrant lemons, highly-specified ceramic implements, and a Lucille Ball-type character, whose single objective is to demonstrate the merits of the mechanism.

A Breeze to Squeeze!

Designed to make a single cup of lemonade at a time, the viewer's interaction with the Lemon-Aider is intimate and voluntary. A juicer fits onto the top of the juicer basin, with two pointed reamers devised to align with the chest of the female character, igniting the use with a subversive implication.

Double the reamer, double the juice!

This juicer and lemonade cart serve as a window into the anxious mind of the hostess, who is a parody of the culturally prescribed ideal woman. The objects become a vehicle for examining heightened domesticity applied to ridiculous domestic problems. The work and resulting use allude to the promise of happiness via convenience by solving "the problem you didn't know you had".

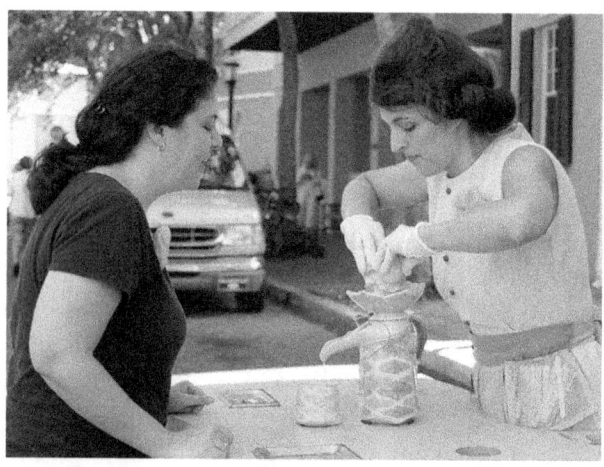

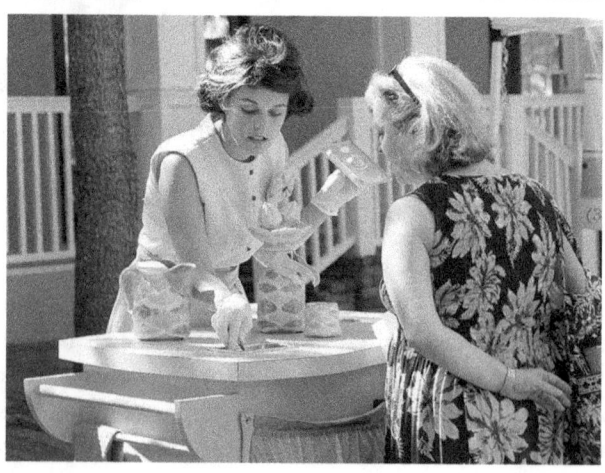

The [Un]Employment Studio

Nicole Seisler

The [Un]Employment Studio is a participatory project
that questions and conflates the value of money, labor, and
the art object. Provided with a pound of porcelain and two
quarters as a mold, participants are invited to work under
contractual agreement at The [Un]Employment Studio on
an hourly basis. During this time, employees use a hand
replication process to make as much porcelain money as
possible, thereby constituting their hourly wage for which
they will be compensated in equivalent US currency. Sets
of the porcelain money are, in turn, sold to collectors
and investors who value the handmade, the time, and the
discipline necessary to produce unique objects.

Employees may sign contracts to make money for
anywhere from fifteen minutes to one hour. If an employee
makes money for one hour, they will be paid the direct
numerical equivalent in minted US Dollars. If they work
for half an hour, they will earn half of the amount they
make; if they work for fifteen minutes, they will earn one
quarter of the amount they make. During an exhibition
of the [Un]Employment Studio, porcelain quarters are
sold for 25 cents each. This money, in addition to grant
funding, is used to pay the wages of employees at The
[Un]Employment Studio. The act of making (and selling)

money facilitates conversations about a range of topics such as employment history and goals, economic struggles, and how we value labor. Most employees report a sense of elation after making money, regardless of when or whether their equivalent minted wages materialize.

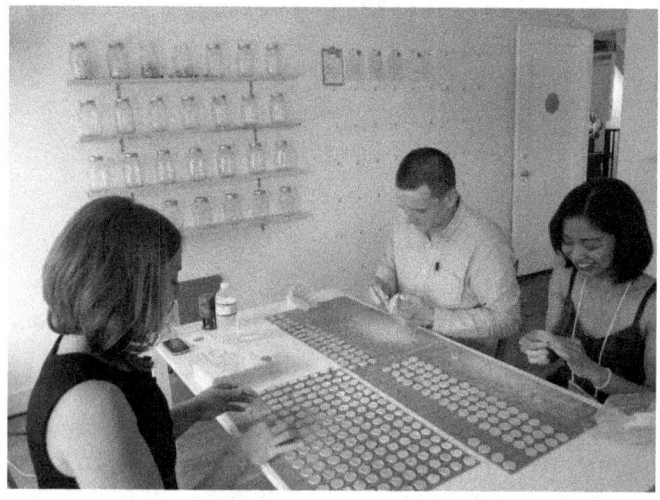

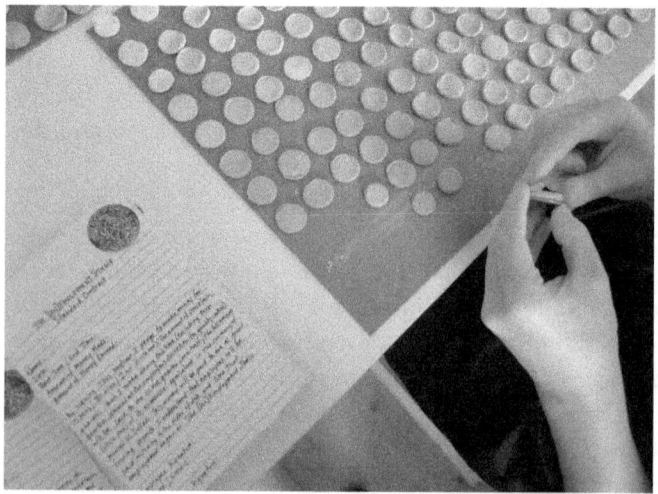

Fargo Sandbag Project

Michael J. Strand

In the spring of 2011, the Fargo-Moorhead region was put on alert to an impending flood that would potentially match the 2009 devastating floods that nearly wiped out the cities that contain a quarter of a million people. In 2009 the city was saved through a collective effort to fill millions of sandbags. In response to this call to action I was interested in how art could be part of improving morale in a community continually called upon to save itself. I imagined the infusion of images and words making their way through the flood fighting process. Imagine... it is cold, late and dark and just as your energy is waning... a pink robot with an encouraging message came through the line to lift your spirits?

The Fargo Sandbag Project was the response and a different call to action. I worked with the city of Fargo to supply 500 empty sandbags and arranged for these to go to grade schools throughout the region. I worked with the Fargo School District and the YMCA system, along with NDSU students and faculty to disseminate the bags and provided a simple process for children throughout the region to draw and write messages of encouragement for those fighting the flood. As this grew I engaged with assisted living facilities, nursing homes, and hospitals to work with individuals who were not physically able to assist in the effort, but wanted to lend their encouragement.

In the end over 9,000 sandbags done by over 6,000 people from 13 states contributed to the effort in just two weeks of work. The bags were deployed into the flood fighting system by the city and just as imagined there were many robots painted on those sandbags, along with rainbows, hearts, cheers and encouragement. Over 5000 of these bags were disseminated into the wall protecting the city, with images and words acting as talismans of encouragement for those filling sandbags, those building the walls and ultimately for the homeowners protected by the efforts of a community coming together.

What Defines Socially Engaged Craft?

The entry point and ability for a craft object to move into cultural systems is as simple as recognizing that "Craft" is not only an object, but also a symbol of human-ness in an increasingly inhumane world. It is the utilization of this potential combined with the inherently participatory nature of functional objects that provides a seamless opportunity to move an idea into culture.

The #Pussyhat Project founded by Krista Suh and Jayna Zweiman as part of the Women's March in Washington D.C. to protest the Presidential inauguration is a perfect example of the relevance of "Craft" in contemporary culture. The project is simply a knitted hat to fend off the chilly D.C air, handcrafted by individuals across the country. Many of these hats are made by individuals who cannot be present at the march. From an aesthetic perspective it is brilliant. A simple knitted form with small cat like ears on two corners has become a cultural icon defining a movement. From a conceptual perspective it is simply, Jedi. The utilization of social media and technology as a pipeline to connect the community of #pussyhat makers with #pussyhat wearers defines the potential of craft in a digital era.

Crafting Words

Juliette Walker

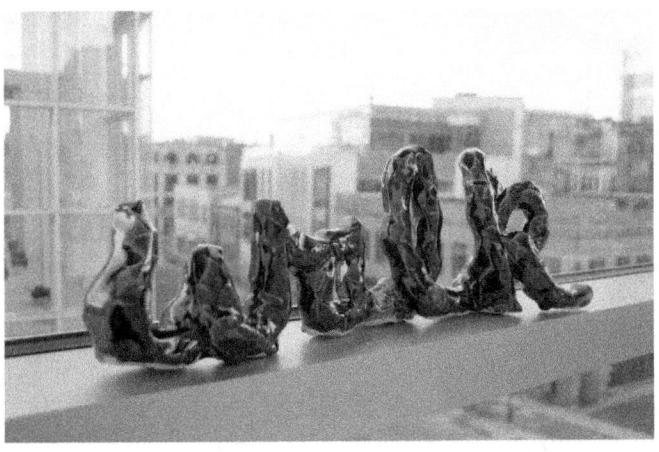

In the spring of 2016, while I was living and working in Madison, Wisconsin, I collaborated from afar with poet Sam Corfman from Pittsburgh, Pennsylvania. Sam crafted words into poems and then I crafted the words into ceramic sculptures. The ceramic poem sculptures were installed at the Madison Public Library and an independently owned bookstore in Pittsburgh called Classic Lines. Throughout the course of the two exhibitions, Sam and I organized poetry readings with our communities. The poetry was activated and experienced through written, spoken, and sculptural forms. By organizing poetry readings, we were able to bring together visual artists, writers and other members of our communities to openly and creatively share with one another.

This project lead to the work exhibited in *Social Objects,* in Portland, Oregon, as well as other projects and explorations focusing on language and words in relation to ceramics, collaboration, and community events. For me, the permanence of ceramics translates into the power of language. The material properties of clay reflect properties of written or spoken words and communication in a really interesting way. My collaborations with poets, writers, and storytellers has allowed for new approaches in sharing projects and encouraged different audiences and communities to be involved.

Conversation with Rachael Disbury

Rachael Disbury currently works as Art and Community Worker at Deveron Projects, a community-focused arts organization in Huntly, Scotland, which runs creative programs that address international issues in a local context. Disbury has an MFA in Contemporary Art from Edinburgh College of Art. She has recently been researching the concept of 'home,' and how arts organizations and artists can create both comfort and opportunities for critical thinking. She graciously shared her thoughts on socially engaged art and craft in an interview below.

JULIETTE: What role does the object play in socially engaged art?

RACHAEL: It depends what you mean by object. In terms of a painting, you might say this is an object and the artwork. In a socially engaged project, there will probably be objects, but they aren't the core of the work, they are part of a wider network. With many of the projects I've been involved in at Deveron Projects, food has been a significant object. What's interesting about this is, with the literal consumption of the object – the meal, the participant is fueled by it; it impacts the interactions and activities of the following hours with the energy spent. That's a very significant role, but there are other factors: the venue, the context of the town, the people invited, the artist and the relationships between. Objects have a significant role but they complement the wider project and can be reused, explored and manipulated, in a way that a static art object might not be allowed to.

JULIETTE: What role does the handmade or craft object play in socially engaged art?

RACHAEL: Socially engaged art is about collaboration, and for me is mostly about relationships between artist and community. This could be completely discursive; it could be discussion, walking events, sharing of knowledge. I don't think the handmade object is exclusively central to socially engaged art. However, it might be central to the artist, and if socially engaged art is about people, then the artist's interest in the handmade object is central.

JULIETTE: Have you had artists at Deveron Projects combining craft and socially engaged practices?

RACHAEL: Last year Deveron Projects planted a White Wood, a living monument to peace. A space with 49 oak trees grown from Joseph Beuys 7000 Oaks acorns, that will grow over 300 years, it embodies ideas of renewal and is promoted as an area for activity and contemplation for the community. The artist who initiated this project is Caroline Wendling and she has an interest in embroidery. Caroline researched the town of Huntly and its connection to linen production. People in Scotland, France and Germany were enlisted to embroider collected quotes of peace in multiple languages in white thread onto white linen, using a Quaker stitch. The flags were to be placed by each of the 49 oak trees. Caroline and myself spent hours with community members embroidering. Stitching together allowed us a chance to talk to a lot of people about the project and allowed them to get involved through an interest, embroidery, that was not initially directly related to the main subject matter of the art work

JULIETTE: Where do you believe the value lies in socially engaged craft?

RACHAEL: 'Craft' is perhaps more suited than socially engaged 'art'. Art is often quite unwelcoming. A lot of the time people have preconceptions of what art means and link it to a gallery, a space they might not necessarily be comfortable in. At Deveron Projects we have no gallery, and prefer to operate within the town. Craft suggests something made with skill and time invested.

Visiting (Belfast)

Summer Zickefoose

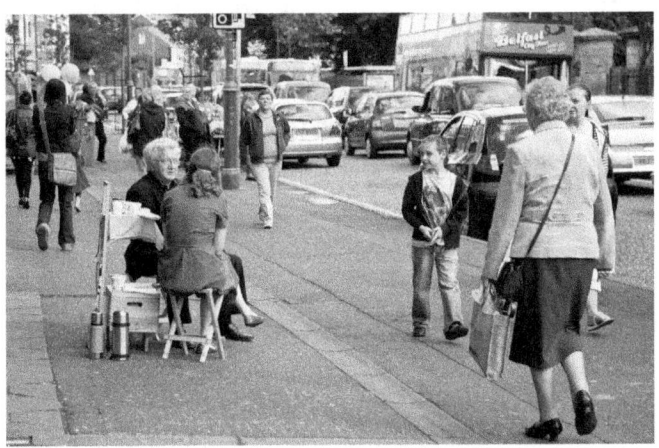

Visiting (Belfast) is a public and participatory project that takes place on various main streets in Belfast, Northern Ireland. The streets of Belfast are juxtaposed with a miniature domestic setting in the form of a portable tea cart used for impromptu conversations between myself and members of the community. The conversations are documented as journal entries written onto the cloth napkins used for the tea, which then act as a receptacle and document of the entire experience.

This small domestic space, in the context of the city's political past, offers the example of building and maintaining community through the simple act of getting to know one another, finding similarities, and engaging in face to face communication. The domestic setting also puts on display the place in which political turmoil is felt most intimately, where family members involved in past violence have been cared for, mourned, and worried about. The dress, table linen and cloth napkins, tea-cart and stools used during the performance, as well as the tea and cookies served, were all handmade and contributed to the gesture of hospitality underscoring the offered conversations.

The crafting of the handmade establishes a value system engaged with time, materials, and design. The value attributed to a guest being worth the effort is felt tangibly in the social environment. While I was offering a gesture of hospitality to the community of Belfast, it was quickly understood that the larger hospitality at play was the residents of the city hosting me. The cultural norms of hospitality entrenched in this tea-drinking culture, where a conversation with a visitor is worth their time, affected every aspect of this project and I am deeply indebted.

What Defines Socially Engaged Craft?

One definition of Socially Engaged Craft is that Craft becomes part of an action and a community. That action may be immediately visible or implied. At times, the action is requested on the part of the audience or user. Socially Engaged Craft is quite often made as one part of a larger social movement or action, and not necessarily made by regular craft practitioners (the Pussyhat Project is one example of this). It does not need to be exhibited and when it is, this can present other challenges in how something active, organic and collective can be contextualized prematurely or rendered still and quiet. Certainly there is always a place for Craft within evolving and shifting political movements. It can provide a peaceful, unspoken and collective image. It can carry powerful meaning via language that may posture as unassuming and familiar.

On Action

THE SOCIALLY ENGAGED CRAFT WORKBOOK

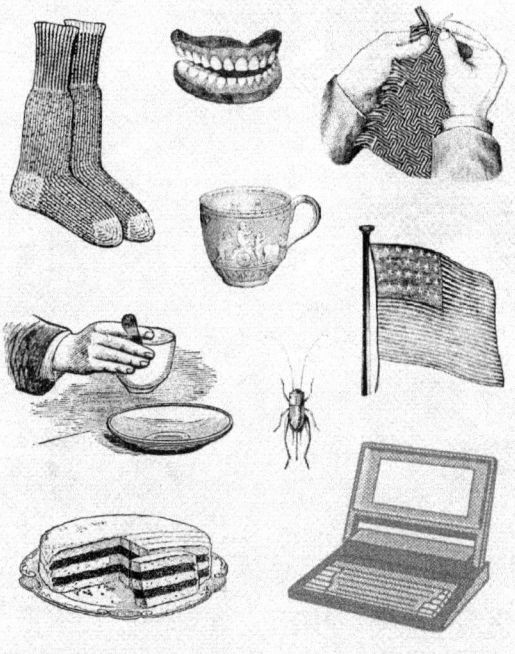

Short prompts, assignments, stories, radical actions, exercises, games, experiments, and interventions that sit at the intersection of craft and social practice. Contributions by the broader socially engaged craft community.

REPRESENTING CULTURAL LANGUAGE IN A SOCIAL DIALOGUE

Alex Amerri

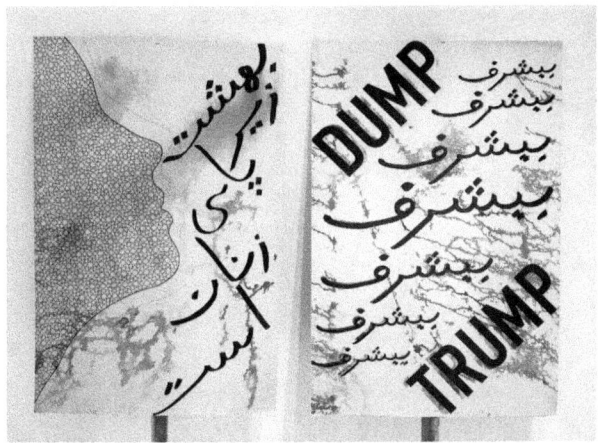

A friend of mine commissioned me to make protest signs for the Women's March in Los Angeles. We decided to make them in Persian, and inevitably they became design studies for upcoming prints that I will be making available. The front is a slight twist on a very common Persian saying that acknowledges how powerful women are in (Persian) society. The back is directed at the chump himself, using the most serious insult a person can place upon another (in Persian society, which values honor and integrity as great as life itself).

How do you choose to represent your own culture's unique voice as part of a larger social dialogue?

LEARNING TO LOVE CERAMICS MORE

The Brick Factory

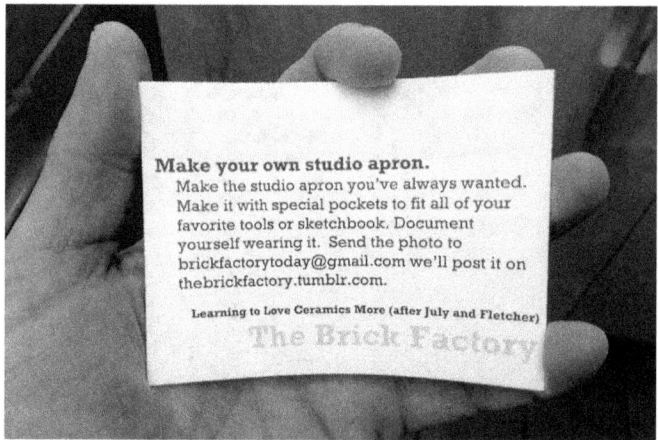

The following are some examples of assignment cards that are The Brick Factory's take on Learning to Love You More with their version Learning to Love Ceramics More (after July and Fletcher), 2011. The assignment cards are meant to be handed out and utilized in a classroom setting or individually and the documents collectively archived. The Brick Factory is Nicole Burisch, Thomas Claude Myers, Erik Scollon and Summer Zickefoose.

Make "Dust Drawings" When no one else is around go to town and clean everything that you can in the shared space of your studio. Don't move anything, just clean around it. Take pictures before you clean, after you have finished cleaning, and later after people have come back and moved their work to reveal the dusty footprint of where things were during the cleaning. These are the "Dust Drawings." Send us before and after pictures, as well as pictures of the dusty shapes of where things were.

Fix a broken piece of ceramics for someone else.
Fix someone else's ceramic object. Leave some reminder of the broken area, such as coloring in the crack or leaving one tiny piece out. Take a picture of this fixed object.

Initiate a conversation about ceramics at a party where there are no other ceramic artists. This conversation can be about anything as long as it relates to ceramics. Either record or write down what everyone said. If it is much later, write down what you remember.

Write a letter to a favorite object you lost. This could be an "I miss you" letter, or maybe you just want to tell the object what's been going on since it has been missing. Send us a copy of the letter.

OBJECT = SUBJECT = OBJECT

Rebecca Chernow

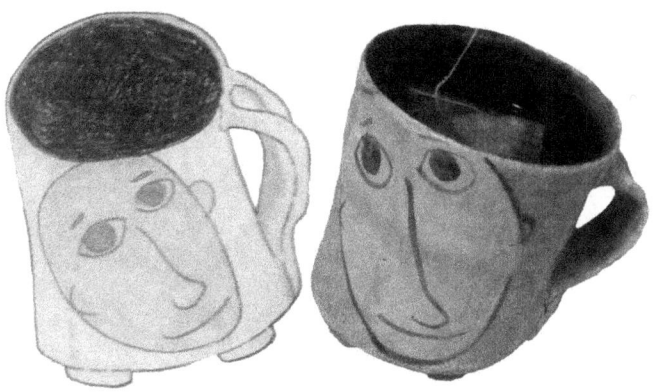

Ceramic mug by John Taylor (2014) and colored pencil drawing
by Becca Chernow (2017)

As craftspeople, many of us are lucky to be surrounded by the handworks of not only our own making, but by our dear friends, mentors, and students.

We use our unique works as currency by trading them and swapping our wares. We gift the products of our skill and time to others that we feel will appreciate them, use them, and hopefully plan on keeping them for a long time. These objects are pieces of material but they are also tokens of the individual that brought them into formation. Either through functional use or everyday admiration, we make a peripheral connection with the maker, all the more so when we know that individual on a personal level.

Assignment
Make a portrait of one of your favorite handmade objects that was gifted to or traded with you that sits in your home, office, or studio. This can be done with photography, drawing, painting,

collage….whatever. It can even be a sculpture of the object itself, like the bust of a Roman emperor.

Remark on the characteristics of the object
1. When did you receive it?
2. How did it come to be in your possession?
3. What do you use it for?
4. How do you know the person who made it?
5. Has its use changed over time (i.e. the frequency of use, its primary function, or has it been broken and fixed?)
6. Has it moved with you?
7. Is it precious or does it get used everyday?
8. Why is it one of your favorite things?

If you are able to, send or give the object's portrait and biography to its maker.

It might just make their day.

HOW MUCH A DOLLAR [REALLY] COST?

Rebecca Chernow

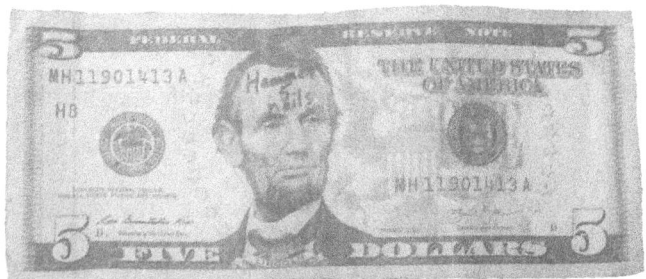

Title from Kendrick Lamar's "How Much A Dollar Cost", from To Pimp A Butterfly, 2015

*WARNING: THIS EXERCISE [may be] ILLEGAL UNDER FEDERAL LAW, so don't say I didn't warn you....

Money is the most social of objects. It is a physical instrument of debt, a store of value, a marker of time, and a moniker of worth. Work is often exchanged for money in the form of hourly income. Reflect on what you do for work, and how you spend your time to earn your money.

Assignment
1. Find a dollar bill of any denomination. It can be a foreign or domestic currency, but you must know the market value of it and be able to spend it in the near future.

2. Write (clearly, but preferably in small print) on the bill exactly what you had to do to earn that specific amount of money. This means that if you earn the living wage in Multnomah County, Oregon at $11.42/hour as a barista, and you've got a ten-dollar bill, you probably made between

thirty and fifty beverages (depending on how busy you get on a typical day) and maybe cleaned a bathroom or a few tables to earn that amount.

3. Now think about what to spend it on.

4. And put your work into circulation

"The price of anything is the amount of life you exchange for it."
-Henry David Thoreau

OBJECTS AND ASSUMPTIONS

Keeryong Choi

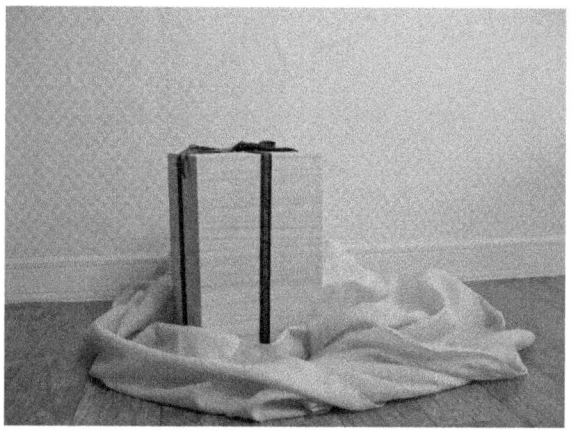

An interview with an individual (gender/male, age group/30-40, occupation/a marketing consultant, nationality/Finish) living in Seoul, South Korea was conducted by the author on 9th of May 2013. The interview provided the author with an interesting insight into his understanding of the local culture that has developed from his encounters, his observations, and experience after more than fifteen years living in South Korea.

For example, he associated the packaging materials, especially the wooden box and dark colored ribbon, with the funeral service (or funeral goods) in South Korea. Although the box and ribbon were used for packaging ceramic gifts or glass honey jars in South Korea, he responded to the package in an unexpected way that reflected his assumption about the particular South Korean funeral culture. As he said in the interview:

"The ribbon on the box reminds me of something like funeral stuff. I do not know if I am correct, but I have seen something like that on television or film. You know, in South Korea, people use black ribbon wrapped around the portrait of the dead. So, I would be wondering what is inside. I would say if I pull out a kind of container-type object, specially made of ceramic or porcelain, I would immediately associate it with an ash-urn and funeral. Although I have not seen anything like that, but I would assume that is how Asians transport ash-urns or the dead. I do not know, maybe in a wooden box or coffin type of thing, like your box with a dark ribbon. One thing is that it does not even have any mark on the surface that indicates what is inside. If it were a container, it would have, maybe, even something like "fragile." Something that kind of message related to what is inside. But, as any visible marking had not appeared on the outside of your box, it made me guess that you do not want to write or you do not want to discuss it. And then, for me, that made me more strongly associate the box with a funeral, like something you do not want to talk about, you know, that can be a kind of taboo in South Korea.

When I saw the contents of the box, I found the combination of the two different materials interesting because it has the ceramic base and top, but then all of sudden, the glass body appears. It is like a kind of contradiction, especially, if you use this kind of 'china'. You know, two thousand years ago, the whole point was, in China, they did not make glass. They made porcelain. In Europe, they did not know how to make porcelain. But they made glass. The shape is like ceramic or porcelain in Asian countries. I think it is kind of mixing the shape and materials or elements in a wrong way."

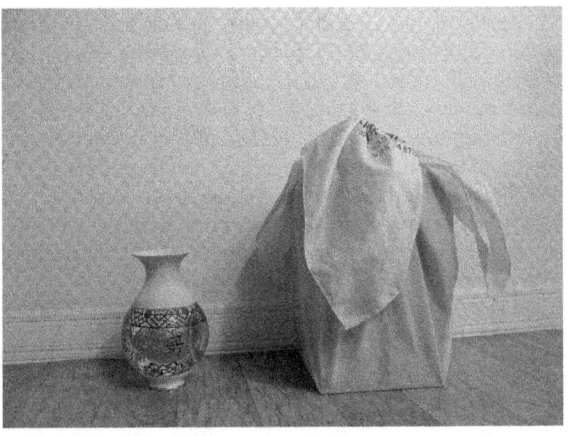

PLEIN-AIR CAKE PAINTING

Roz Crews

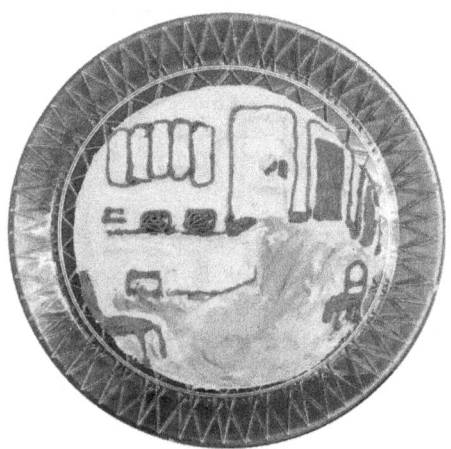

My father grew up working in a bakery with his dad in Florida, and I often think about all the things he might have learned in the bakery— about baking, about patience, about precision, about community. When I was a kid, he used to show me cake stands, frosting tips, and special plastic decorations from their old shop, and I dreamt about the giant vats of swirling sugar. When I found out my parents would be in town, I automatically wanted to figure out a way to include them in the Intro to Art and Social Practice class I was teaching, so I wrote this assignment about site-specificity, patience, new mediums, and relationships. It was nice to share cakes, to share family, and to participate in something totally weird.

Assignment
Site-Specific
Plein-Air Cake Painting
Inspired by Erin Mallea and Plein-Air Painting

Overview
Each participant will make a cake, decorate it with a scene from the art building, and give the cake to someone in the art building. Professional cake decorators should provide guidance.

Instructions
- Bake a cake and bring it to the gathering with other participants.
- Select a comfortable location somewhere in the art building where you can use frosting to paint a scene on your cake; approximately one hour.
- Determine who you will give your cake to.
- Give away the cake to someone in the building.
- DOCUMENT!

Presentation
Explain what you painted, what the experience was like, who got the cake, why.

HENRY JAMES HAVER CRISSMAN'S PROJECT DEVELOPMENT WORKSHEET

Henry James Haver Crissman

This worksheet may serve as a handy reference for site specific participatory projects. Helping to highlight inequities within a project's structure while keeping focus on the gestural qualities which allow these actions to operate as art.

****

This first set of questions does not need to be answered in any particular order.

*) Whose project will this be? Establish the terms of authorship up front. Are you working with a collaborator? With a group? Is there a hierarchy?

*) Identify the location. What opportunities and materials are there? What is the history of the place? Will that history influence the context of the project?

*) Identify the audience. Who will be there? What is their history? What are their needs and wants? What are their interests?

*) What are your assets? What do you have to offer?

****

The second set of questions expands on the first set of answers. Connect your observations and develop a project.

What is the intent of the Project? How does it serve you? What service does it provide?

What will be the role of the audience? (spectator, participant, voluntary or involuntary performer, co-author) What is the expectation of them? What do they provide? What do they receive in return?

How will audience members know to become involved? What cultivates interest in the project? (spectacle, advertisement, intervention)

What places you in the position to offer this? Does your socioeconomic situation impact how we should understand the value of significance of the project?

How do the resources, collaborators, audience members, and assets come together to create a conglomeration whose value is greater than the sum of its parts? In what way does this project operate as an art work?

What happens afterwards? What is the role of the documentation? Are there issues that should be addressed in the reproduction of images from the project? Does documentation askew the reality of the project?

Now give 'er a great title go and undoubtedly fail!
But when you do, fail beautifully. ;)

YOU'VE BEEN NOTICED

Jamie Crooke Powell

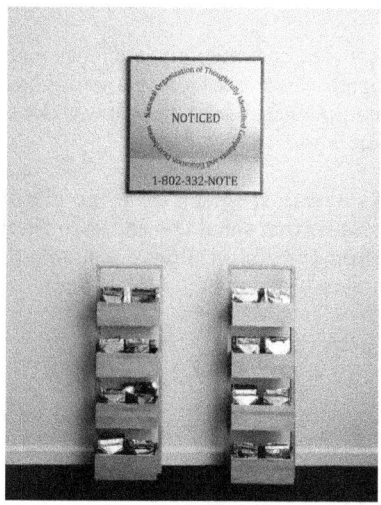

The interactive installation, "You've Been Noticed" is a hypothetical organization that aims to address the very real psycho-social needs of individuals in our particular culture and time due to violence, racism, and inequalities.

The acronym N.O.T.I.C.E.D stands for the National Organization of Thoughtfully Identified Complaints and Education Distribution.

The project, "You've Been Noticed" was developed by myself to directly address the recent violence, hate, racism, and fear that this current election has produced and exposed. Many people are suffering from two distinct interpersonal conflicts: fight or flight. Some people are ready to fight the blatant violence, hate, racism, and fear; while others need a moment of healing first. As a trained artist that has also studied therapeutic modalities Jamie is sensitive to the many individuals who are trying to negotiate our current socio-political climate.

The goal of this project is to use principals from therapeutic practices, such as mirroring and witnessing, to sincerely offer a moment of relief and reflection, while using a hypothetical national model for an advocacy group or campaign. The project will record complaints anonymously that will be posted on the project website for others to read in an attempt to realize that none of us are alone in our feelings of anger, grief, etc., and it is possible to continue positive change in this country.

Participation is welcomed by calling the phone number (802) 332-6683 to release your comment or complaint. You can specify if you would like it to not be listed, as the process is the work.

You can view the resources that were available in person by visiting the project website.

www.NOTICEDproject.com

ART AND THE PRACTICE OF COMMUNITY

Jen DePaolo

The practice of love is the most powerful antidote to the politics of domination. - bell hooks

Hand made objects and shared meals have a long lineage in my family and it's no wonder that I've become a potter and a cook, serving meals on hand made pottery both in and out of the gallery. Since my 2008 MFA exhibition, Home Economics, I've been exploring the way traditions, habits of consumption, land-use and material culture shape human lives and the landscapes that bear the burden of industrial production. I've come to see small-scale local production as a necessary form of resistance and as the greatest good a community can offer it's own place and the world at large.

Faced with a changing climate, a polluted planet, global warfare, economic disparity, national divisions and concentrated power, it's hard to know where to start as a socially engaged artist though we have plenty of fodder.

Referring to times like these, Toni Morrison says "This is precisely the time when artists go to work. There is no time for despair, no place for self-pity, no need for silence, no room for fear... That is how civilizations heal."

So we set out to heal our civilization. No biggie.

I believe socially engaged craft asks us to be present to our humanity. It teaches us empathy. Socially engaged craft may allow us to grieve, learn and celebrate. This action counters what Pope Francis calls America's "unbridled capitalism". Being a socially engaged artist allows me to love my community through the food, objects and experiences I help create.

In his recent Poem on Hope, farmer, activist and writer Wendell Berry implores us: "Hope then to belong to your place by your own knowledge of what it is that no other place is, and by your caring for it as you care for no other place…"

For the last 12 years, my place has been Albuquerque, New Mexico. I am still getting to know this place and how to care for it. I am learning the names and shapes of the fish that have disappeared from the Rio Grande through a community art project called Collective Memory. I've learned about the many cultures that have shaped what we now call New Mexico through my work with a ceramic mosaic project that has covered the Albuquerque Convention Center in this narrative history.

Albuquerque is a creative and collaborative city that does much with little. We rely on each other to share resources, leverage support and build networks. Our artists are responsive to and reflective of each other- more cooperative than competitive. In the years since my MFA exhibition I've been gratified to find a community of growers, vintners, chefs, writers, dancers, musicians, poets, event planners, marketers, community organizers and other artists who are happy to work together. Together we've made beautiful things happen on farms, in galleries, in shops, on street corners, in shelters and in community centers and we're committed to growing this work in the years ahead.

About the Author
I partner with Edible Magazine editor Stephanie Cameron to curate pop-up meals on handmade pottery. We serve locally grown and produced meals, and incorporate dance, music, poetry and art.

Stephanie and I promote events, connect with local growers and producers, and envision future collaborations. Each fall, we share a general proposal with a wide network of potential partners. We coordinate team meetings throughout the winter, garnering feedback and ideas from all involved. Our final events are participatory and multi-faceted.

Our guests enjoy unique experiences that are shaped by our land and the people that care for it. Our events are not passive. Guests are asked to share stories, follow prompts, meditate, collaborate on poems and interact with the growers and makers that surround them.

WARM UP EXERCISE FOR EXPLORATIVE MOVEMENT

Monica Dixon

Find a clear space you feel comfortable moving in by yourself or with a friend. If at home, consider moving furniture to make more open space.

Create a playlist of songs that lasts the amount of time you have to devote, anywhere from 15 minutes to an hour. Start with music that makes you feel calm, gradually building to more energetic songs if you desire.

Wear clothes that are comfortable, along with something extravagant or costume-like that feels distinctly different from your day-to-day identity. This could be a mask, wig, scarf, or something more elaborate.

Give yourself permission to be silly, weird, child-like, playful, obnoxious, and corny. It is impossible to make mistakes with this exercise. The intention is to explore sensation and possibility through movement. Let go of any need to judge or filter yourself.

Take as much time as you wish with the following prompts, allowing yourself to explore variations and follow tangents:

As the music begins, start lying on your back. Close your eyes if it helps you bring your attention inward.

Listen to the music.
Notice patterns.

Imagine the sounds as shapes that are moving through and around your body.

Notice if there is anywhere in your body that you feel a strong reaction to a particular rhythm or beat.

Extend your legs and arms upward.

Bring awareness into your joints, circling ankles and wrists. Let the movement spread to your knees and elbows like you are crawling or dancing on the ceiling.

Roll yourself onto your belly. Allow yourself to move against the floor, massaging out any tightness or tension in your legs, belly, arms, and face.

Make your way to your hands and knees. Feel the length of your spine. Explore the range of motion.

With the music, visualize the sounds as shapes moving you from the head to the tailbone.

Shift your weight onto your feet, slowly making your way to standing.

Continue experimenting with motion. If you find yourself stuck in thought, let yourself move repetitively (such as swinging arms from side to side or shaking). When you're ready, you'll naturally break out of the repetition into a new pattern, finding new and unique ways to move in response to sound.

How to know if you're a socially engaged craft artist

Jeni Hansen Gard and Forrest Sincoff Gard

Check all boxes that apply

☐ Do you like working on projects with other people?

☐ Do craft materials, processes, or traditions appeal to you?

☐ Do you make things with your hands?

☐ Is it important for you to know how and why something was made?

☐ Are you interested in building or strengthening community?

☐ Do you thrive on negotiating boundaries and exchanges?

☐ Are you making objects with the intentions of using them?

☐ Are you always wondering about the afterlife of art objects?

☐ Do you sometimes feel your work doesn't fit in?

☐ While in the studio, do you find yourself daydreaming about making work with others?

☐ Are you an activist at heart?

☐ Do you want to challenge the craft status quo?

Congratulations! If you checked 5 or more boxes you may be a Socially Engaged Craft artist.

Continued on Page 131...

A CALL FOR THE SOCIALLY ENGAGED CRAFT BIENNIAL

Shannon Hebert Waldman

Craft practices and objects have long been used in social practice works, but it has not been until this moment that makers have reclaimed their work within the social practice realm. Socially Engaged Craft artists follow a tradition of antagonistic practices against the institution as a tactic of social engagement. However, the field of SEC is already institutionalized with exhibitions such as the Makers Biennial at the Museum of Arts and Design,[1] Queer Threads at the Leslie Lohman Museum of Gay and Lesbian Art,[2] Disobedient Objects at the Victoria and Albert Museum,[3] Spaces of Production at the Center for Craft, Creativity, and Design,[4] and now Social Objects at the 2017 NCECA. Conferences that focus on Socially Engaged Art, such as Open Engagement, now actively include conversations expanding to Socially Engaged Craft. Those making within this field have begun to consider how to exist within institutions while maintaining the integrity of their commitment to community building through and beyond the institution.

Contemporary makers are producing their objects as the bases for effective community building both within and without institutions while continuing their aim of addressing social issues for a variety of stakeholders.

To create a sustainable connection between Socially Engaged Craft and the institution I propose a continuous base for the emerging field of Socially Engaged Craft through a biennial exhibition: the Socially Engaged Craft Biennial.

The Socially Engaged Craft Biennial would highlight contemporary makers involved in social engagement through their craft practice. Each maker will directly involve the community surrounding the locale of the biennial in their Socially Engaged Craft practice in addition to an exhibiting their work.

The Socially Engaged Craft Biennial would prompt important questions about Craft's involvement in discussions on the socially engaged works of contemporary makers. The works proposed for the Socially Engaged Craft Biennial would serve as interactive objects that bring awareness to, create community around, or directly address social issues. Many of the display strategies and programs will be designed to serve the interactive needs of the objects as well as to host sites for conversation and community based making.

A focus on a select number of makers whose practice is grounded in Socially Engaged Craft is ideally suited for extending the practice into a concentrated community. The balance created between the interactions of the maker with the visitor and the activation of the gallery space through objects relating to these interactions will demonstrate how Socially Engaged Craft can exist within an institution while maintaining its integrity in active community dialogue.

The strength of a biennial is that it puts into practice a long term commitment to Socially Engaged Craft. The most effective Socially Engaged Craft practices are those that allow for long-term evolution with reflection and evaluation.

Endnotes

Yunza, Jake, curator. "NYC Makers: The MAD Biennial." (2014). http://madmuseum.org/exhibition/nyc-makers (accessed 1.21.2017).

Chaich, John, curator. "Queer Threads: Crafting Identity and Community." (2016). https://www.leslielohman.org/about/press-release/2013/queer-threads-pr.html (accessed 1.21.2017).

Grindon, Gavin and Flood, Catherine, curators. "Disobedient Objects." (2014). http://www.vam.ac.uk/content/exhibitions/disobedient-objects/ (accessed 1.21.17).

Zapf, Marilyn, curator. "Spaces of Production." (2015). http://www.craftcreativitydesign.org/spaces-of-production/ (accessed 1.21.17)

A PROMPT FOR THE PROSPECT OF ACTIVATED OBJECT PERMANENCE

Brian Gillis

Objects have power. Whether related to a solitary or shared experience, objects contribute to the way a body exists in the world. Objects are solvents and sinks, catalysts and beacons, radiators, archives, projectors, lubricants, amplifiers, resistors, engines, salves, mills, multipliers, conduit, fluxes, and stabilizers, etc.

Object Permanence is the understanding that objects continue to exist even when they cannot directly be observed. This fundamental psychological concept, first conceived of by Jean Piaget concerning cognitive development, will serve as the foundation to consider the potential for a power loop between an object and a body.

Some steps to realize activated object permanence:

1. Thinking of all the possible ways objects afford engagement and the cooperative transfer of power, find an object that in someway speaks to something you feel you should be doing but aren't.

2. Take at least five minutes to behold this object. What does it look like? What does it feel like? What is it made of, from, used for, set in relationship to, etc.? How does it meet the world (sit, stand, lay, roll, hover, etc.)? Objectify it. Think about this object as something that in and of itself is not just representative of that thing you should be doing, but also understands why you haven't/aren't doing it. Personify it. Think about this object's nature, the various contexts it has, is, and could exist in. Think about this object as something that has the capacity to give and draw power. Think about this object as that which is of the world but needs your agency to be active in it. Think about all of the possible permutations of this object in the world, physical or other, rational or other, real, imagined, implied, etc. etc.

3. Wear this object in some way that is concealed, but you are physically or psychologically aware of. This can be the actual object or a photograph of it. It can be in a pocket or taped to the body, exist as a 2 Dimensional image drawn on the body, sewn into clothes, ingested, tattooed, implanted etc. etc. etc.

4. Put yourself in a situation that requires you to do that thing you think you should be doing but aren't while being at least faintly aware of the presence of the object.

PLAY WITH CLAY INITIATIVE

nicole gugliotti

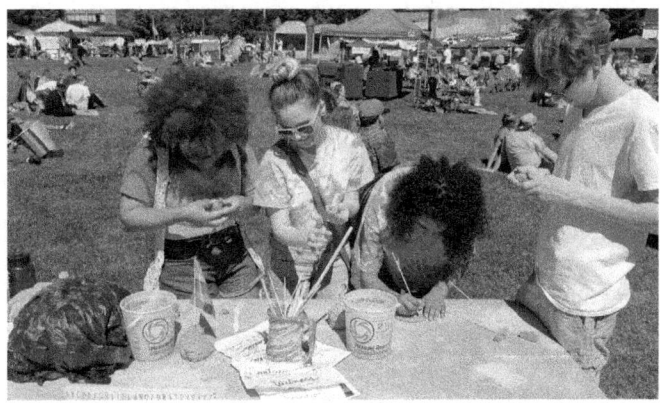

Over the last year there has been an incredible amount of national and international tragedy. The murder of Alton Sterling and Philando Castile, the Pulse night club shooting, and the Syrian refugee crisis, just to name a few. The lack of control we have over some things and the urgency to protect each other and make progress can feel overwhelming. It's easy to believe that the world we live in is a terrible place. There is certainly plenty of injustice that needs our attention and fighting it is very important work.

It is also important to play, to be with people doing something light. This could mean recharging or making space for connection and new ideas to crop up. The Play With Clay Initiative's (PWCI) goal is to provide communities, art spaces, schools and individuals with the resources to create space for folks to come together and play with clay. We want to encourage people to engage in play, to do something with their hands and to make objects as a backdrop for discussion.

Assignment
Organize your own Play With Clay event

Materials Needed
Wet Clay
Table (maybe some canvas to cover it)
Humans

How To
Show up somewhere there are humans in need of play. Put clay on a table and invite folks to play.

Optional Materials
A discussion prompt: "How are you feeling?" "What vessel can contain what is happening?"
Some basic clay tools
Letter stamps

When you're done, you can share photos and details of your event on our website.

playwithclayinitiative.wordpress.com

HONOR A GROUP

Holly Hanessian

Honor a group that is working on behalf of social justice, working on behalf of the environment, or working on behalf of others: teachers, sanitation workers, and lower tier health-care workers. Many of those fields make little money and our society disregards their value. Making them feel valued by giving them or sharing a handmade moment with art adds human value to their life.

My students invited local Beekeepers over for desserts made with local honey and served them on pottery made for the occasion this last December. The Beekeepers were very honored knowing that we had considered their work, acts of community and environmental service.

SWATCHES

Gregory Hatch

A series of prompts to have you consider the textiles around you during intimate moments.

Conversation starter: What profession related garment do you think is the sexiest?

Think of the last time you were intimate with someone(s). What clothes were you wearing? Now think of another place you wore one of those pieces of clothing.

Conversation starter: Is a terry cloth towel clothing?

When you see a stranger wearing the same item of clothing as one worn by a past sexual partner, compliment the stranger.

Start to keep track of the patterns your sexual partner(s) wear. Write down your findings in a notebook.

Conversation starter: If you are still wearing socks, are you naked?

THE DEMOCRATIC CUP: LISTEN WITH THE INTENT TO UNDERSTAND

Ayumi Horie and Nick Moen

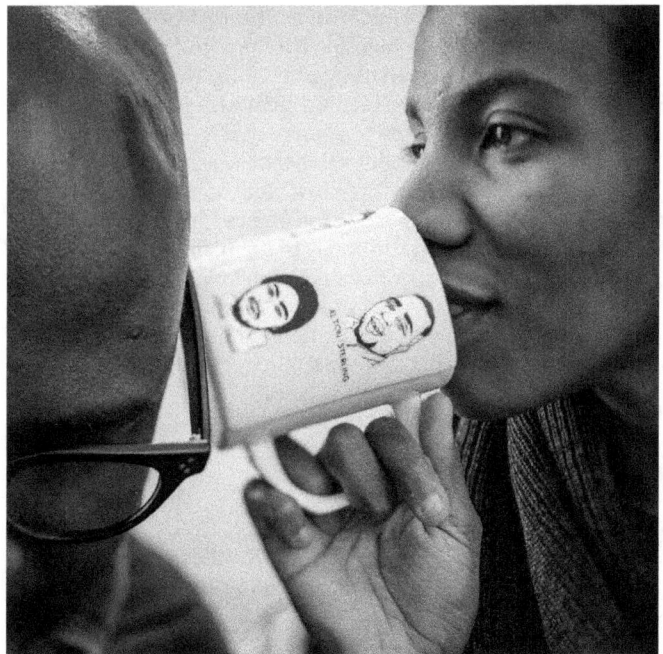

Photo credit: Sean Alonzo Harris

Requirements
- 3-5 participants with varying political views
- 1 Democratic Cup

In this exercise, each participant will act as interviewer and inter-viewee in an open-ended interview chain. The Democratic Cup will serve as a relay between participants in the form of a hot cup of coffee or tea. Person 1 will interview Person 2, Person 2 will interview Person 3, etc… until it loops back around to Person 5 interviewing Person 1.

This exercise is about listening with the intent to understand your partner's point of view, without responding with your own views or opinions. The challenge rests with the interviewer/listener to keep an open mind and allow another to truly express their concerns and positions without the threat of antagonism or hostility. We hope that participants will come away from this experience more connected to their cohorts and open to having additional conversations, the next time with a balance of talking and listening.

Steps
1. Find someone with dissimilar political views than your own.
2. Make them a hot drink using the Democratic Cup.
3. Interview that person using a cup from The Democratic Cup project as a conversation catalyst. Your goal as the interviewer is to listen to your interviewee and learn about their positions without feeling the divisive binary of being 'anti' or 'for'. Try and listen in a more holistic way. Try to listen to hear, not to reply. Ask open ended questions.
4. Taking the Democratic Cup with them, the interviewee finds a different person with dissimilar political views and repeats steps one and two as the interviewer.
5. Repeat steps one to three until a cohort of three to five people is formed. Close the chain by having the last interviewee interview the first person.
6. Debrief with all members of the cohort and discuss how your views have shifted, expanded or solidified.

Suggested Questions
1. Tell me about the image on the Democratic Cup and how it relates to your political views?
2. How do your political views differ or align with your family and what in your life has influenced those positions?
3. What position of the current administration do you support or are concerned about? Please use personal events to further explain your points.
4. How have your political views and opinions influenced choices in your life including your career, partner, or geographical location?
5. How can we work together across political differences?

This exercise is inspired by Celeste Headlee's Ted Talk *10 Ways to Have a Better Conversation*

REPLICATE AN OBJECT

Max Infeld

Make a replication of an object your friend has. Just use existing materials you have. Replace with said object.

-brought to you by your friends at The Replication Machine.

DAILY RITUAL JEWELRY

Joshua Kosker

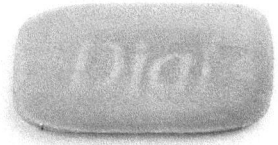 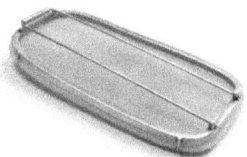

In order to make "daily ritual" jewelry, you'll need to:

1. Find an object that has been transformed through a daily ritual, routine task, and/or has a direct connection with the body and everyday life (i.e. bathing implements, food, tableware, bedroom items, etc).
2. Make it wearable so that it can be reconnected to the body in a new way that adds meaning to the object and the wearer.
3. While making the work, reflect upon the initial process used to transform (and original function associated with) the object.
4. Once the piece is made and the jewelry is placed on the body, the object should lose its original function, but not its associations with the physical/sensual experience of the daily ritual.
5. Wear the jewelry.

WRITE A LETTER IN THE FORM OF AN OBJECT

Kari Marboe

Think of someone you admire
Write a one page letter
Read aloud
Make long list of observations
Dissect and record as many elements of a letter as possible
Write your letter again, but this time in the form of an object

PROJECT CANARY

Mac McCusker and Project Canary (nicole gugliotti, Lauren Karle, & collaborators)

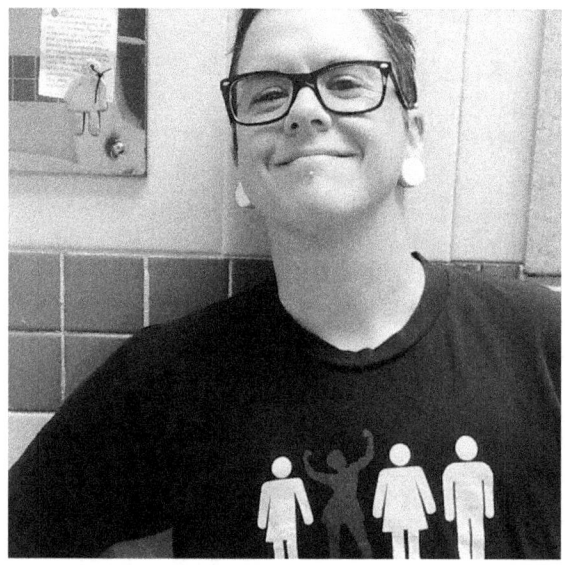

Project Canary uses craft as the vehicle to spread stories of injustice – racial, gender, immigration status, reproductive justice, religious, and other human injustices. The goal is to empower those whose voice is often unheard, making politics real. The project honors experience above rhetoric by connecting people to each other through their individual stories.

Last year as part of Project Canary, I made a ceramic gender neutral figure in several sizes and then created press molds of the figure to replicate it. The figures were made into magnets, key chains, necklaces, and pins. These were left in bathrooms, gas stations, and welcome centers across the country in response to the bathroom bills. Some were stamped with "Repeal HB2" and those were placed in rest stops across the state of North Carolina.

An attached tag directed the finder to the Project Canary website where they could read the story that inspired the object. This simple art object created the potential for conversation.

How you can participate
- Example 1: Read stories on the Project Canary website.
- Example 2: Write and anonymously submit your story.
- Example 3: Make objects, code them with a story number and place them in your community.

How it works
1. Project Canary has a growing collection of stories written by people who have experienced injustice. Each story is submitted anonymously and is assigned a number.
2. Artists then make small objects inspired by the stories and the story number is inscribed into the artwork.
3. Objects are placed in the community for people to find. A tag is attached to the objects directing the finder to the website where they can search the story number and read about the story that inspired the artwork they now own.

Visit our website to read/submit stories and get details on making your own.

www.projectcanary.org

DO IT TOGETHER

Lauren Moran

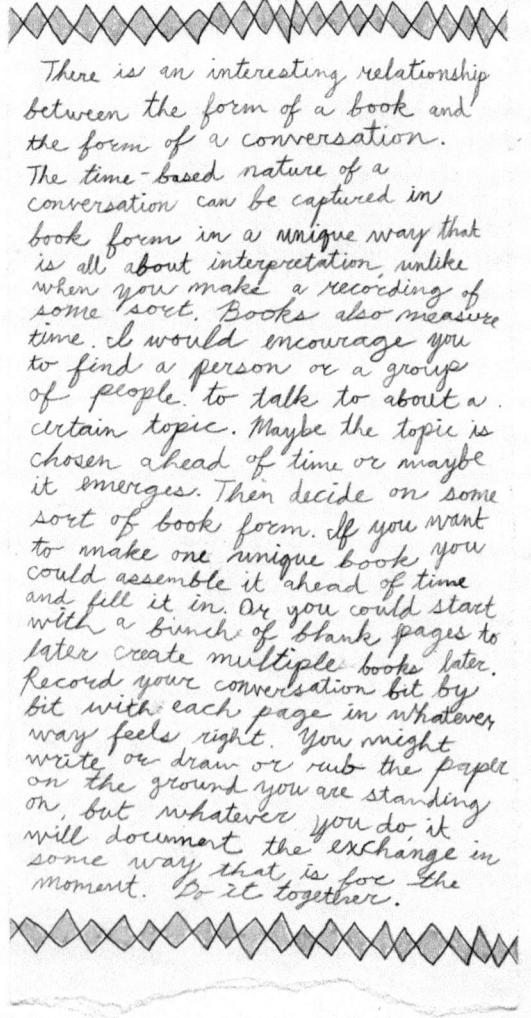

There is an interesting relationship between the form of a book and the form of a conversation. The time-based nature of a conversation can be captured in book form in a unique way that is all about interpretation unlike when you make a recording of some sort. Books also measure time. I would encourage you to find a person or a group of people to talk to about a certain topic. Maybe the topic is chosen ahead of time or maybe it emerges. Then decide on some sort of book form. If you want to make one unique book you could assemble it ahead of time and fill it in. Or you could start with a bunch of blank pages to later create multiple books later. Record your conversation bit by bit with each page in whatever way feels right. You might write or draw or rub the paper on the ground you are standing on, but whatever you do it will document the exchange in some way that is for the moment. Do it together.

A PROVOCATION FOR DIGITAL CRAFT

Hannah Newman

Perhaps the most social objects present in our daily lives are our connected devices—computers, smartphones, tablets, etc. New digital tools compress the whole world—an infinity of information—into the space of physically manageable, personal devices. How can these social objects be used within the context of craft?

Our first conception of the word craft traditionally brings to mind handmade objects. The intentionality and deliberation of creating an object by hand has long served to create connection between maker, user, and object. In The Practice of Everyday Life, Michel De Certeau supposes that much creativity within modern society comes from the daily actions of consumers, or users, who adapt and re-contextualize readymade items that are available to them for their own individual purposes, needs, and tastes. Could craft be considered the daily actions and creative impulses of individuals who re-direct the prefabricated goods and tools available to them?

Social media is a readymade tool or structure for communication, performing a variety of functions from advertising to conversation, public dialogue to inside jokes—interpersonal and mass communication. How might these functions be tweaked, altered or otherwise engaged with in order to initiate more inviting, provocative, or engaged interactions within digital mediums? In what ways are people already modifying these readymade forms to individualize, beautify, and enhance their daily lives and communications? As humans engage the digital, many opportunities exist within digital processes for imagination and disruption. What new forms of (inherently social) craft wait to be discovered within the context of platforms like emails, text messages, gifs, or Instagram photos?

With their innate design for connection, social media and connected objects seem uniquely poised to perform the vital functions of craft—enriching, improving, chronicling, and claiming our lives and our space.

AUNTIES AT CRAFT

Salty (Xi Jie Ng)

Once I helped manage a project at a senior activity center in Singapore that served low-income seniors in a neighborhood of flats. Elderly females or "aunties" at the centre had, for many years, a strong craft practice going on that was a kind of cottage industry. Applying simple sewing methods on donated fabric, they made tissue box holders, pouches, baby bolsters, pillows and other paraphernalia, drying discarded beansprout husks from a nearby supermarket to use as stuffing. The star item was quilted blankets made by hand; each one could take weeks to accomplish. A typical day at the centre would see them hard at work in small groups. Some of them would be there from morning, while participating in the center's many activities like exercise or outings. They never took a cent from the sale of the items and did this doggedly as a kind of hobby.

The artist, herself female, facilitated a process where the aunties were invited to share life stories, conceptualise a design and make a fabric collage quilt of their own. In our culture, ladies from the older generation seldom think of themselves as creative or having a unique identity, and it was challenging for them to come up with something special that told a story. One recalled the food carts that went around when they were children; another focused on creating something pretty with flowers. Perhaps riding on existing social dynamics, a few of the aunties displayed some level of competitiveness, complaining that the artist was paying more attention to others. Some grumbled that they would rather be home watching their beloved drama serials instead of being obligated to the centre management to be there, and a couple nearly walked out of the project from these tensions. Simultaneously, some of them were getting pretty intense with their quilting and reported having insomnia from thinking about the project, or waking up in the middle of the night to sew.

When the project was finally completed, each of them seemed to beam with a quiet pride, yet groused about the imperfections in their work, claiming it was "not as beautiful" as others'. During the presentation party, they sat in neat rows and took turns coming to the front to take a photo with the artist, who by then had developed an endearingly intimate, semi-frustrating relationship with the older ladies. The largely quantitative evaluation required by the funding institution was limited because the aunties' responses to the questions were often monosyllabic, or appeared to be neutral without going further into why it was enjoyed or disliked, perhaps for diplomacy's sake. A nice project summary video, which I oversaw, was made so the funding institution could show something to itself and the public.

After all that, many of the aunties returned to the crafts they had always executed with confidence, enjoying the comfortable repetition it afforded. A few of them tried coming up with more creative designs for quilts. Even today, once in a while someone tries to teach everyone a new kind of fabric craft they can replicate. I recently bumped into one auntie and her husband, who told me he found her sewing till late at night, "wasting electricity." This man was often the lone male sitting quietly amidst the cacophony of women, next to his wife. He would read the newspapers or just relax.

I think projects like that can never really be evaluated quantitatively; honest evaluation requires anecdotes that do not shy away from the struggles of the group so as to present a happy picture of a community art project well done. The video was certainly useful in giving a very basic sense of the project but could not, due to its instructed parameters, delve into some of the more fascinating things that unfolded. Impact is lived experienced, and while there must be an attempt to relate it, the futility of this exercise should be acknowledged. The main thing I took away from this project was my friendship with the aunties. I ended up volunteering at the centre for a time and years later, still bump into some of them around the neighbourhood. The cottage industry is still running. I wonder if it brings them some kind of fun that had been missing or lacking in their lives. And because many of them were housewives, perhaps the crafting group feels like a kind of workspace they never got to experience, with colleagues, hard work and results, ensconced in the tactility of fabric, lost in a quiet, self-affirming work that makes skipping a drama serial episode worthwhile.

DIG CLAY WITH A TOOL MADE FROM CLAY YOU DIG

Rosa Novak

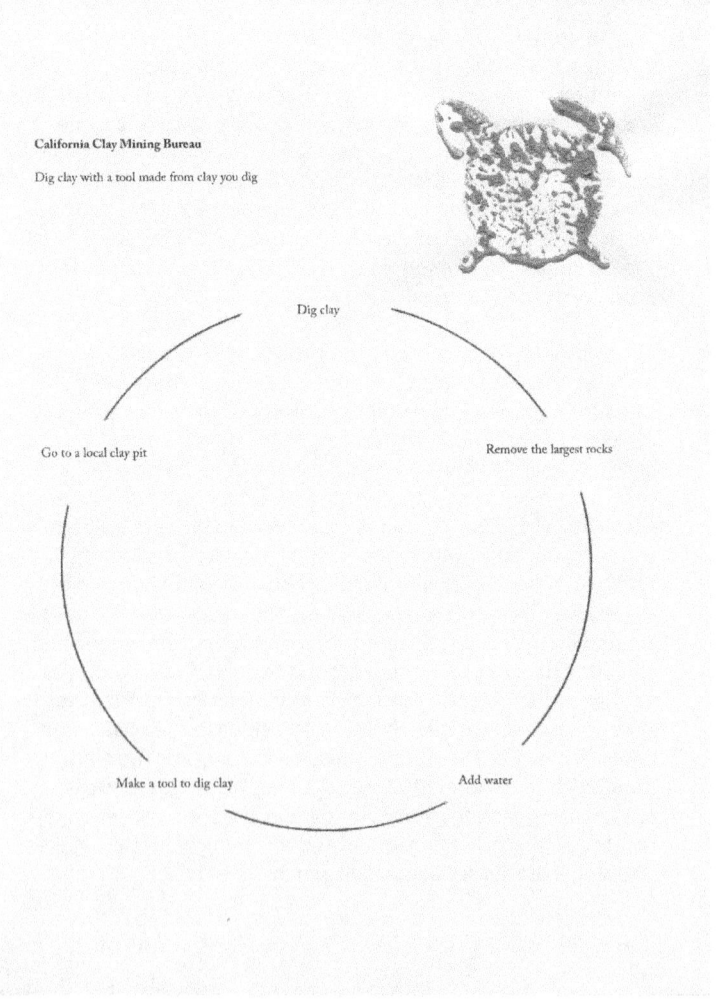

California Clay Mining Bureau

Dig clay with a tool made from clay you dig

Dig clay

Go to a local clay pit

Remove the largest rocks

Make a tool to dig clay

Add water

WITH JUSTICE FOR ALL: TEXTILES FOR PEACE AND SOCIAL HEALING

Iviva Olenick

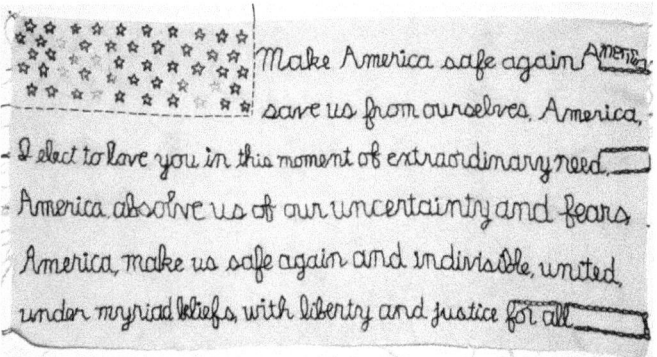

Your banner/your thoughts;
Your flag/(y)our rights;
Your sign/your body

To craft your own Textile for Peace, you will need plain cotton muslin or, if fabric is not available, a shirt, a pair or pants or even a bed sheet you're willing to reclaim; a needle and thread in a color visible on the fabric; a message to share with friends and even strangers.

Not sure how to embroider? You can improvise stitches, using a basic running stitch (in–out/front–back) to start. YouTube has great stitch tutorials, or you can substitute fabric markers for needle and thread. Like the look of the American flag? Adapt it to your message and visual sensibility. Want to honor your heritage from another country? Try adapting that country's flag into a new version, which will include your originally authored words.

Not sure of a message? Think of song lyrics you cannot forget;

chants from marches that energized you; the words of politicians you admire or fear. Use these as a starting point to author something powerful in this climate of fear tactics. Use this exercise of handcraft and word-craft to clarify what you most care about.

Once you've made your flag, stitched t-shirt or hand-written jeans, call a group of friends. Read your message. Have a friend record you and share the video or photographs on social media. Spread the Textiles for Peace movement with people you love and those who will most benefit.

CRICKETS AND CLAY

Lauren Sandler

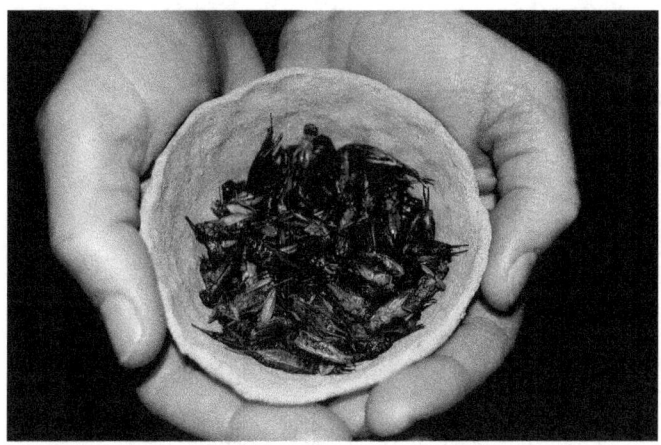

Who
Beginner to Advanced Students

Materials
You will need harvested clay, tools to dig and prepare clay, a pound of edible crickets, and basic ceramic tools.

Actions
- We harvest clay and catch crickets from a local suitable area. Edible insects may also be purchased.
- Students build vessels for edible insects.
- Together we share a community meal of roasted crickets in sculptured containers.

Conversation
- Students explore the dynamics of food insecurity and inequity, sustainable practices, and literal and figurative nourishment.
- We discuss the journey from seed to belly in food production, and from mud to pot in clay production.

Questions
- What are the origins and travels of our food and our clay?
- How have vessels changed historically, across cultures as a result of migrations, colonialism, and industrialization?
- How do technologies and methods of food cultivation, preservation and storage influence vessels?
- Do we select a vessel for aesthetic, functional, cultural, political, economic, and/or personal reasons?
- How are vessels intersections of multiple ideas and actions?
- What is the position of the artist in the modern mechanization and corporatizing of food and clay?

Investigation
- Students research vessels made for particular foods across histories and cultures.
- Students share images and sketches of their vessel ideas.
- Examples include fondue pots, tagines, bento boxes, mitad, and mortar and pestles.
- Students discuss the experience of eating crickets, and the cultural, political, economic, health, and environmental impact.

Goals
- From nutrient-rich soil with insects that thrive, to vessels that store and serve, to a community that sustains, we explore the multifaceted ways clay provides nourishment.
- Through this process students consider our environments as sources of food and clay.
- We learn to prepare workable material and understand the characteristics needed to formulate   clay bodies appropriate to our vessels.
- This project illustrates the clay cycle, and makes transparent our contemporary food chain, from earth to mouth, and earth to ceramic piece.
- The inquisitive nature of the experience calls for a willingness to consider unforeseen possibilities.

Resource information
- Entomophagy is the practice of eating insects.
- Eighty percent of the world eats insects.

25,000 YEARS

Michael J. Strand

In 2012 I lectured at the social practice conference, Open Engagement, about my work at the intersection of craft and emergency management. While waiting in line for a potluck style dinner, a graduate student from a California institution asked me what I do. After I explained that I am primarily a potter he proceeded to ask what pottery has to do with "social practice". In a rare moment of succinct clarity I reminded him that 25,000 years of participatory history is quite an advantage as one does not have to invent an entry point into the hands, hearts and minds of those you wish to engage.

EDITING WIKIPEDIA: INCREASING PRESENCE OF FEMALE, TRANS & GENDER NONCONFORMING CRAFT PROFESSIONALS AND ARTISTS

Robin Tieu (& Art + Feminism)

In Toronto, Canada, on March 19, 2017, the Gardiner Museum will be hosting an edit-a-thon with the intention of increasing the low representation of female, trans and non-gender conforming Canadian ceramic artists, craft practitioners, designers, scholars and historians into Wikipedia's database.

The event will start with a public discussion on the topic with guest artists Janet MacPherson and Helen Cho, moderated by Karine Tsoumis, curator of Gardiner Museum. Students from the Ontario College of Art and Design University, Sheridan School of Craft will be participating in this project to increase and expand upon Wikipedia's entries.

You Can Host Your Own Event!
"Art+Feminism's goals are two-fold and symbiotic: to close the gender gap in both content and participation on Wikipedia.

According to Wikipedia's only study of its user community, less than 10% of Wikipedia's editors identify as cis or trans women. Studies have also found that new female editors are more likely than male editors to have their edits reverted.

The gap is not just quantitative, but also qualitative: The famous example from a New York Times article a few years ago is that is that a topic generally restricted to teenage girls, like friendship bracelets, are only a few paragraphs long while topics that are typically associated with boys, like toy soldiers or baseball cards, have multi-page entries with chronological lists and so on. Other studies suggest that articles about women are more likely to link to articles about men than vice versa. Furthermore, articles about women frequently use gendered words like "woman," "female," or "lady" while articles about men rarely use words like "man," "masculine," or "gentleman."

What this means is that while the reasons for the gender gap are up for debate, the results are not: the content is skewed by lack of participation.

The lack of gender equity in the art world is also well documented. According to some studies, while 51% of artists today identify as cis or trans women, only 27 women are represented in the current edition of H.W. Janson's survey, History of Art, up from zero in the 1980s. And although half of the MFAS granted in the US go to women, only a quart of solo exhibitions in New York galleries feature women. So, before we even get to Wikipedia, women are already at a disadvantage in the art world.

But, this is where you can help. Because Wikipedia is open access and open source, the tools are in your hands. There are lots of ways you can help close the gender gap on Wikipedia. There are numerous WikiProjects that focus on women artists, women in science, women in sports and so on. Next time you are on Wikipedia, consider making a free account to start editing articles. Not sure how? Visit our website for videos and tools to get started.

Art+Feminism can help you to host your own event, learn to edit, and network with others doing the same!"[1]

Resources
Watch Videos on Learning to Edit on the project website.
www.artandfeminism.org/editing-kit/

Check out Wikipedia pages that need editing.
wikipedia.org/wiki/Wikipedia:Meetup/ArtAndFeminism/Tasks

Endnotes
1.   Art+Feminism, "Art+Feminism Introductory Lesson Plan 2017,"
        Art+Feminism accessed February 19, 2017. http://www.
        artandfeminism.org/editing-kit/

BEAR IN MIND

Brian Widmaier

a bear's service is not a garden's lover...

Please always try and make things better but bear in mind that

All you need is the best intentions and your great ideas.

Talk talk talk. Tell people what they need. Don't ask.

Work, work, work with people that you consider less privileged than you.
Everyone needs someone richer and smarter to show them how to be happy.

Talk talk talk to people you already know and like
(and people that might give you money.)

Use use use social media to convey your message.
Really it's the best way to reach out to others.
Anyone who doesn't follow you does not matter anyway.

Never ever ever commit to a solid plan or physical meeting.
I mean really...let's just Skype when we both kinda have the time.

¯_("-)_/¯
I'll text you.
xoxo :)

Always think outside the box.

Implants only have the ability to enhance.

1,2,3,4
Change will happen within a month, max.
A gold gold golden rule be be be...better to be lonely than be with a fool.

Leave your audience...confused?

For inquiries about speaking engagements please email bwidma@gmail.com

Interested in Socially Engaged Craft? Learn more:

What is Socially Engaged Craft? Find out at:
sociallyengagedcraftcollective.org

I want you to know about socially engaged craft.
Visit sociallyengagedcraftcollective.org
to find out more!

What is Socially Engaged Craft? Find out at:
sociallyengagedcraftcollective.org

I want you to know about socially engaged craft.
Visit sociallyengagedcraftcollective.org
to find out more!

What is Socially Engaged Craft? Find out at:
sociallyengagedcraftcollective.org

I want you to know about socially engaged craft.
Visit sociallyengagedcraftcollective.org
to find out more!